how to
FIND A JOB
START A BUSINESS

by Donald R. Brann

FIRST PRINTING — 1981

Published by

EASI-BILD DIRECTIONS SIMPLIFIED, INC.
BRIARCLIFF MANOR, NY 10510

Library of Congress Card #80-65878

NOTE:
All metric dimensions are shown within 5/100 of a centimeter.

Due to the variance in quality and availability of many materials and products, always follow directions a manufacturer and/or retailer offers. Unless products are used exactly as the manufacturer specifies, its warranty can be voided. While the author mentions certain products by trade name, no endorsement or end use guarantee is implied. In every case the author suggests end uses as specified by the manufacturer prior to publication.

Since manufacturers frequently change ingredients or formula and/or introduce new and improved products, or fail to distribute in certain areas, trade names are mentioned to help the reader zero in on products of comparable quality and end use.   The Publisher

BE A WINNER

From early childhood through most of our adult life, we fight a continual war for survival with somebody, something or some situation over which we have little or no immediate control. In youth, many discover the kind of job they want is hard to find, even harder to hold. A desire for success, a willingness to put in a full day's work, invariably creates animosity among those goofing off. Goodwill and good intentions are subject to group pressures. Loners invariably become targets for all who prefer to be "joiners." Year after year we face problems that flow from an ocean of sources. To live a way of life many only dream of living, consider these factors:

... Problems invariably breed fear, a period of crisis.

... Crisis frequently represent a turning point.

... Accept the fact that conscious problems will fill a large part of each day and particularly those hours you owe to others.

... View each problem as a challenge, one that offers instant opportunity. Each solved insures more time to live with one less.

... Strive to be a participant, a producer, an individual who continually makes contact with people, places and things.

... Learn to continually nurture new interests, coexist with rancor, jealousy and especially lamebrain leadership.

... Divide your mind, energy and each waking moment into separate and distinct spheres of activity. Invest as much time as your job requires but make a daily investment in an endeavor that broadens your area of activity.

... Learn to search out, listen and follow good advice. It is in very short supply.

... Only you can control your destiny. Improve your use of time and you create a valuable asset-YOU.

Don R. Brann

TABLE OF CONTENTS

Lend Fate a Helping Hand

Walk into any bookstore and you see dozens and sometimes hundreds of HOW TO books that promise something for everyone. Make a million in your spare time . . . find peace of mind through prayer, meditation or diet . . . learn car repair . . . bricklaying simplified . . . enjoy sex more frequently . . . lay ceramic tile, and many, many others. Each promises what many seek.

HOW TO books are special. While publishers of fiction, biography, anthropology, psychology and other scholarly subjects frequently stimulate the sale of many a lemon by printing flattering quotes in clever advertising, do-it-your-selfers develop a sixth sense. Unless the author includes all the direction and offers same in words and pictures that insure success, word gets around and sales take a dive.

The author of this book has been specializing in HOW TO since the thirties when he applied the idea of a dress pattern to lumber and created Easi-Bild full size woodworking patterns. Like most Depression born new business endeavors, it started on a shoestring investment in space that rented for $12.00 a month. When pattern customers discovered they could successfully use a pattern, hundreds started building and selling lawn chairs, rocking horses, then tackled construction of one, two and three bedroom houses from easy to follow directions.

Finding a job and/or starting a business requires direction plus on site job experience. You can gain this without leaving home. You can also apply for a job offered in classified advertising, seek help from an employment agency or counselor, or do as many have regrettably done, invest hard earned savings in buying a franchise operation.

Everyone who finds it difficult to get work or hold a job believes it's something personal. A black feels it's because he's a Negro, a Jew because of his religion, yet Catholic Irishmen kill Protestant Irishmen with less reason and logic. Color and religion lose their sting when an individual begins to pull his or her weight in every endeavor that benefits others who participate.

Learning a skill at home and becoming sufficiently adept to do the same work for others requires only time and effort. You gamble no capital other than for living expenses, tools and material. If you lack tools and material, practice in an adult education class. If you lack self confidence, do as directions suggest, help someone do what you want to learn.

In easy to follow, step-by-step direction, this book and the more than fifty others in this series show each reader how to find work they can do well and earn good money doing it.

Youth living in depressed areas can find meaningful work when they follow the directions offered. Retirees find a satisfying use of time while a successful executive, living under great pressure, discovers instant relief from tension and hope in the future. All can accomplish this magic with no capital investment, no blue sky franchise operation. Regardless of age, sex, color, social or economic background, this book can help everyone find their true potential.

How individual action shapes each life was clearly illustrated in a series of three letters the author received some years ago. These came from a long term prisoner in a state penitentiary.

In his first letter the inmate wrote to say he had begun reading the bookcase book in the prison library but, due to limited time allowed, wondered whether we could please send a discarded copy he could study in his cell. Having no funds, he couldn't even pay postage.

8

Months later a second letter expressed his thanks and explained how he had made a scale model. This gave him confidence. It also focused his mind on doing this kind of work on release.

He discovered a simple fact of life relatively few take the time to recognize, i.e., we instinctively fear doing something we have never done before. When he realized construction of a handsome built-in or free standing wall to wall bookcase actually begins by drawing a line across the ceiling and dropping a plumb bob down from this line to the floor, it took the fear and mystery out of the work.

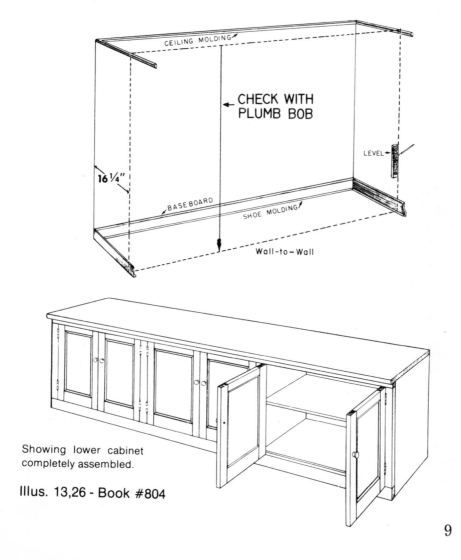

Showing lower cabinet completely assembled.

Illus. 13,26 - Book #804

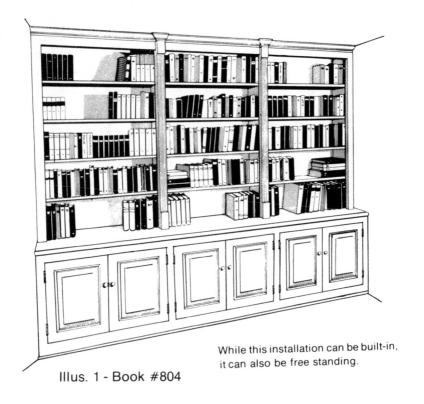

While this installation can be built-in, it can also be free standing.

Illus. 1 - Book #804

Several years later, a third letter, still signed by the same number, explained he was on parole and was determined to stay that way. On release he had applied for work in a home improvement center. During the interview, he showed the scale model, explained how he learned cabinet making and how much he liked doing this work. By an odd coincidence, the interviewer had recently completed a handsome set of lawn furniture following directions offered in another Easi-Bild Book.

When asked what wage he expected, he promptly responded, "Pay whatever you can afford." His frankness in revealing his past, his willingness to work and to accept whatever sum the employer could pay, clinched the interview. The letter went on to say that after two very happy and productive years on this job, he left to start his own business. It closed with this, "Thanks to that book you mailed me years ago, I am now, at 48,beginning to live the kind of life I should have lived the past 30 years."

10

Just recently the author received similar letters from another state prison inmate. He requested a copy of the kitchen modernization book which he too had been reading in the prison library. When permitted to build scale models in the workshop, the warden asked if he wanted to help build cabinets for the prison kitchen. The experience gave him new confidence, direction and hope. On release he wrote to say he immediately got work modernizing a kitchen for a member of the parole board and how each satisfied customer helped him find another.

His letter, like those from many readers, described how the books also simplified installation of a kitchenette in a garage, basement and attic used for living. Creating income producing living space offers many new job opportunities.

Book #758* provides floor plans for six different kitchens, plus all essential information needed to level up floors, etc. It not only explains how to build conventional base and wall cabinets, but also designer styled cabinets and pole type furniture that is as popular with apartment dwellers as homeowners. All material specified is readily available in most home improvement centers.

Recessed cabinet doors, a built-in oven, sink and range have great appeal. These cabinets and those shown on page 12 and 20 can compete with the best available.

Illus. 1-Book #758   *also #608,658

Through the years the author has received hundreds of letters from readers who took the time to describe how good direction helped create a new activity and provided new hope in the future. All agreed, the author's promise, "Anybody can do anything, if they follow direction," was fulfilled in their case. To insure success, each book assumes the reader has never previously done any of the work, and explains each step in words and pictures that every reader can follow. In 55 titles and 8020 pages, each starts at A and goes completely through to Z to eliminate all coldspots. This not only builds self confidence, but also encourages amateurs to turn pro.

Illus. 5 - Book #758

One inch square tubing and prefinished plywood, plus direction that TELLS ALL, insures professional results. When cabinets are installed over a ceramic or quarry tile floor as described in Book #606, it generates a conversation piece and attracts many more customers.

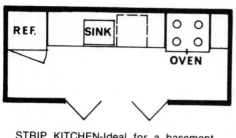

STRIP KITCHEN-Ideal for a basement, attic or garage conversion to living space.

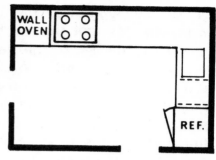

The L KITCHEN (shown above) and the U KITCHEN (below) are to be found in most houses built during the forties, fifties and sixties.

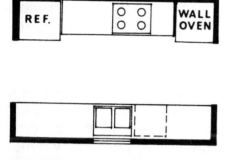

PULLMAN TYPE KITCHEN is popular in the rehabilitation of abandoned buildings.

Illus. 8, 9, 10, 11-Book #758

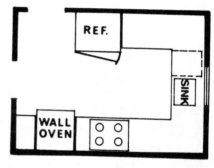

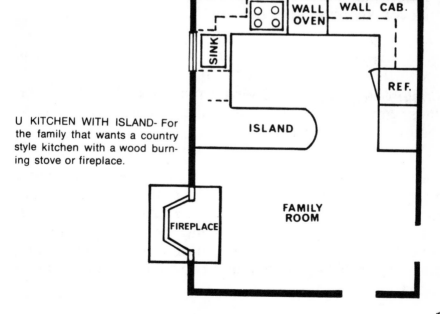

U KITCHEN WITH ISLAND- For the family that wants a country style kitchen with a wood burning stove or fireplace.

No one really knows what the future offers, what jobs they will get or how long they will be able to hold them. Thousands put in a full day's work, are happy with their job, only to have a regulation come out of Washington that puts the company out of business. Only you actually are in control of your destiny. Only you can exert the needed effort to change pace and direction. Those seeking work must continually condition their minds to the possibility of change, continually expect the unexpected. In the beginning, getting and holding a job is like finding your way through a dense forest. In some places you may find a path and make progress. Then years later, through conditions over which you have no control, you are back in the woods with no path to follow.

Everyone who continually searches finds something. It may not provide the income or status of what they did in the past, but it does keep them occupied until something better materializes. Many others have created an image they refuse to abandon. Like movie and TV stars who rate a good review, then believe their own publicity, losing an image frequently creates serious mental problems. How we appear to our family, friends and neighbors is a mirage many refuse to abandon. Learn to accept change. Take any work you can get while you keep trying to get what you want.

Your inheritance of time is limited. Hitting the bottle or pills only destroys whatever time is left. Many healthy, intelligent people begin to die in their twenties, thirties, forties and fifties, when they refuse to shift their mental gears and do whatever work is available.

Learning to make a simple plumbing repair like changing a faucet washer, opening up a clogged drain, as explained in Book #675, can help establish a magnetic field of activity. Making a meaningful contact, doing each job at a price the customer can afford, provides an opportunity to do many other jobs for the same customer, providing you are willing to learn HOW.

14

A customer with a constantly running toilet, faulty wall outlet or ceiling fixture, a clogged gutter or leader, or a hundred other problems most homeowners continually face and don't have the time or physical capability of solving, generates vibrations. When you solve one problem, many will ask you to solve others. Before long you become an important part of that household. When you develop this rapport with one person, you can develop the same meaningful contact with hundreds of others.

HOW DO YOU GET STARTED? If you live in an area filled with abandoned buildings, you go one way. If you live in a suburban area, you go another. Every job and new career requires making contact, a personal appearance. Explain what work you can do and immediately offer references as to your honesty and willingness to work. Don't wait to be asked, offer same. Bear in mind one facet: YOU MUST MAKE CONTACT. People are conditioned by daily happenings, by financial problems, by local crime. All are magnetically drawn toward those who can solve a problem.

Every physically able retiree needs something to do. The myth of retirement, as a means of enjoying life, seldom delivers what it promises. An executive between jobs must also analyze his or her physical and financial need and take immediate action. Those with limited funds must accept the fact that they can no longer maintain their current standard of living. Each must act as decisively as a surgeon using a scalpel. While searching for work, invest every spare hour in a physical effort that relieves mental pressure. Preconditioning one's mind to these facts of life helps justify developing a "survival insurance program."

Selling or renting a home you can no longer afford, while spending every available hour rehabilitating an abandoned building, transforming a garage into a rental apartment or building an addition for the same purpose, can save a mind, a marriage and a home. The experience invariably proves so richly rewarding many decide to do the same work for others.

15

Letters from readers continually report the therapeutic and economic benefits. One executive added a second story to a two car garage and created an apartment as explained in Book #763. The work provided escape and helped alleviate anxiety. On completion, he had no difficulty renting it to a young couple who soon became his good friends.

Another letter described how a new government regulation forced one manufacturer out of business. The heartbreak of seeing over 30 years of his life go down the drain drove him into a deep depression. To compound the negative, his favorite daughter was divorcing her husband. To create separate living space for the daughter and two grand-children, he decided to build an addition. Working from Book #609, he had no trouble adapting the step-by-step directions to building a much larger addition. The work took almost a year, a year in which he had no time to think about anything but the next day's work. As the addition neared completion, his lawyer discovered flaws in the regulation and he decided to go back into business on a limited scale, now a stronger, more experienced individual.

Everyone who attempts to build a garage, addition or rehabilitate an abandoned building welcomes honest help. Much of the initial work is manual labor. As the work progresses, each step provides an education in all building trades. You learn how to build and install base and wall cabinets in a kitchen, lay ceramic tile in a kitchen or bathroom, etc. Each job attracts many others.

To fully appreciate who you are and what the future offers, remember these basic facts. Everyone needs a place to live, food to eat, clothes and transportation they can afford. This is the fabric of life that creates buyers and sellers of most needed services. Finding a job requires providing one or more of these needed services or products.

Fear of failure and one's pride frequently destroy initiative and effort. Even those who should know better, who have enjoyed a measure of success, frequently fall apart, lose confidence and chicken out to a bar stool rather than face a series of discouraging job interviews. Since no one knows what the future offers, unless you continually make an effort and TRY, you can get lost fast.

Consider loss of a job, fear or failure as stepping stones to a brighter future. Learning to reshape that image you see in the mirror each morning is a miracle only you can perform. Just as the mind of an unborn child invariably inherits certain fears, phobias, strength and weakness from one or both parents, only you control your destiny. Where you were born is a circumstance that can only shape a small part of your life. If and when you mature, you should take full command. To illustrate this point, consider the number of mature years you considered yourself "all thumbs," because you were unsuccessful building a footstool in grammar school.

The nation currently faces enormous change. This provides unlimited opportunity for many, great despair for others. What happened in the past invariably surfaces in the future. Become a doer in any area that appeals, and in every area where you can render a service someone wants.

To fully appreciate the depth of current change, consider what has happened to the automobile industry. The power struggle between management's ability to manage, and labor's determination to run the business, has created more car recalls in 18 months than the total the industry experienced in over 50 years. While not everyone is mechanically inclined, every able bodied, normally intelligent individual can learn to make a good living specializing in those repairs and parts replacements millions of cars require. Every gas station that pumps gas and offers car repair provides opportunity. Watch a mechanic change spark plugs, oil, a filter and you soon learn the basics of analyzing and making more sophisticated repairs. You may start by pumping gas and discover by helping a skilled mechanic, you are far more mechanically inclined than you imagined.

If a service station or auto repair shop needs help, and only offers a minimum wage, it offers a profitable investment of time. Within X months, you could become a first class mechanic. If you recognize the potential in this approach, go to a library and borrow a repair book on the model cars that repair shop specializes in. While you will ultimately need to buy a copy for ready reference, only consider buying a How To book after you have read it to make certain the author explains every step in words and pictures you understand.

Know Yourself

In the twenties when radio first became an important means of communication through to the early fifties when TV made a much deeper penetration of the mass consumer mind, millions have become accustomed to liking or disliking a certain commentator, program or personality. Prior to radio, the newspaper columnist had cultivated this area and built sizeable followings. But few had so deeply penetrated the mind or shaped the thinking of so many so quickly as TV and radio. These two mediums made it relatively easy to sell anyone anything. Among the easiest to sell are those hungry for the prestige and independence of owning their own business. Thanks to radio and TV, more franchise operations have been sold to more innocent suckers than during any period in history. Industrious souls, who worked a lifetime building a nest egg, buy a business with no previous experience. And thousands now find bankruptcy the only way out. Regardless of the service or product, never invest a penny until you have worked for the company or one in the same field for at least a year. Even though you only earn a minimum wage, the experience and savings are worth the investment of time.

Offering everything you ever dreamed of having, fast buck salesmen have mesmerized thousands into setting up franchise businesses that require borrowing money or investing life's savings. During the eighties, the rate of bankruptcy among these franchised operators will establish a new record of failure.

This book only attempts to cover the kind of business and/or new job opportunity that can be started with an investment of time and sufficient funds to cover one's living expenses. How long the reader should stay in the field selected depends entirely on the progress that develops. A youngster who offers to wash cars and renders a satisfactory service faces little difficulty selling the same customer a polymer finish waxing job. Those who decide to replace worn screening soon discover they can make even bigger money selling the same customer an intrusion proof,* heat saving, double window. The same customer can frequently be sold a "termite proofing" job as explained on page 144.

Making contact is the key to finding a job or starting a business. Read this book and select an area of interest. Talk to retailers who sell the products you will have to buy to render this service. Since they benefit everytime they help you find a customer, many will help by posting your name and services on a bulletin board.

Those with no money for material can still obtain a basic understanding of each trade. Additional skill can be gained by building scale models of kitchen cabinets, wall to wall bookcases, outdoor furniture, etc. Those with no tools or place to work can get practical experience in an adult education class. Those who TRY and follow DIRECTION that explains HOW soon discover fate lends a helping hand.

---

*No window is actually intrusion proof. The double walled polycarbonate panels require an intruder to use a wrecking bar or hammer to enter. Since this takes time and creates noise, few burglars take the risk.

Modernizing a kitchen not only provides job opportunities, but also enables a homeowner to make a long term investment, one that generates a sizeable Capital Gains. Offering to do part or all the work establishes a Positive Point of Contact.

Directions suggest measuring overall length then dividing space to build equal size cabinets. Since most kitchens vary in size, directions recommend various types of cabinets, along one, two, three or four walls. The sink and dishwasher cabinets can also be built to fill available space.

Inquire whether there is a music lover in the family. Suggest installation of a ceiling speaker to be connected to a stereo system as explained in Book #612. Crime is on the rise so suggest installation of the wiring contacts and bells needed for a burglary alarm as detailed in Book #695.

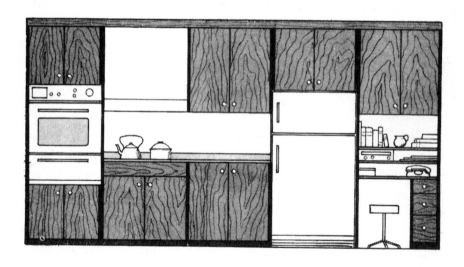

Built in wall oven, counter range, refrigerator and desk offer one very acceptable plan. Directions also suggest installing a cleaning cabinet in place of the desk.

Illus. 7 - Book #758

Since one's thinking can be shaped by external forces and experience, many erect imaginary fences around those areas of activity where a previous effort resulted in failure. As problems multiply, we instinctively withdraw to smaller and smaller circles of activity. We neglect to realize one's capabilities, like the hands on a clock, are constantly changing. What we couldn't do in the past is often easy to do when we find and follow good direction.

While no one really knows what the future holds, most good luck stems from one single source. Find a need and fill it. Another way to discover your personal potential is to solve problems. Every problem you solve creates positive vibrations that power forward movement. Every step forward creates new and larger problems. Accept each as a step up the stairs to good fortune, and you soon sit in the sunshine of success.

When we appreciate God's gift to each consists of time and energy, and this inheritance is ours to use as we please, we realize why some few are far luckier than others. Why some win fame and fortune, while others never leave first base.

Consider these basics. At birth we receive a body, a brain and time. How we invest or spend our inheritance and use our brain determines where, how well and long we will live. How we use our body determines our physical health. You may enjoy good health, possess an average or brilliant ability to think, but until you begin to do what needs to be done, you seldom reach or enjoy your true potential.

In childhood the use of time is dictated by others, but as we mature, and "do our thing," what we do shapes that someone called you. Medical research has proved no two individuals are alike, that each has a separate and distinct combination of genes and rarely do two individuals actually use time in identical ways. Those destined to live the kind of life others only dream of living, inevitably gravitate toward a formula consisting of time and effort that works like magic.

We live in a strange and perilous age. Man's ingenuity, intelligence and imagination have enabled him to rocket to the moon, yet millions can't find or hold a job or get a night of peaceful sleep. All too many spend countless hours spinning their mental and physical wheels while sinking deeper into despair, drugs, crime, alcohol and divorce.

From the moment a newborn baby starts nursing at its mother's breast, to the instant life departs, its needs must be supplied by others. In every economic and social level, we are all both buyers and sellers. How we relate, how we make contact to others' needs, how we convert time into the currency needed to pay for all needed services, determines where and how well we will live. Learning to cope with life's daily problems continually requires direction and a willingness to do what needs to be done.

From early youth through most of our golden years, we assume a problem is something negative, when in reality, it's a source of great power. And like every form of energy, learning to harness this power necessitates making contact with both its negative and positive elements. Every rags to riches Horatio Alger story emphasizes the manner someone, no different physically or mentally than yourself, harnessed adversity to rocket to success.

Those fortunate enough to have been born during the years when all children's stories started with the words, "Once upon a time," can recall many favorites the TV generation never listened to. As children, we were encouraged to believe everything was possible. If anyone could learn to sing, swim, ride a bike or go from rags to riches, so could we. All we need do was play in the fresh air, breathe deeply, eat our spinach, and try, try, try. Try was the magic password.

In bygone years, people took time to live, raise a family, cultivate friends, build a home, a marriage and a career. Today we live in a different time zone, one that requires making split second decisions. Unless we swerve right instead of left, go around a darkened area instead of through, we gamble on survival.

This book is an inanimate object that generates positive vibrations. It explains how the Impulse Power, inherent in every problem, can be harnessed to provide solutions you can afford. In easy to follow step-by-step direction, it tells how to put worry to work, how to solve mental, marital, physical and financial problems. It explains How To get the kind of work you enjoy doing . . . start a part or full time business with no investment other than living expenses . . . get a peaceful night's sleep without popping a pill . . . live a way of life you previously only dreamed of living.

Think of this the next time you switch on TV and spend countless hours dialing around a wasteland of nonsense, or equal time worrying about a problem only time and effort can resolve. Learn to put worry to work. Worrying is a mental habit we cultivate early in life, one that grows and wastes more of our inheritance than we realize. Worrying can be likened to spinning your wheels in a snow bank or slippery surface. This raises air pressure. It can blow out a perfectly good tire as fast as a problem can cause you to lose your cool. We don't suggest breaking the worrying habit, but harnessing it.

Remember — every thought you conceive, every move you make, is fueled by particles of time and energy in the same way gasoline powers an engine. Invest spare time developing a service, a product, making repairs or improvements, or in a time consuming hobby, and you begin to learn how to live, how to double the purchasing power of a tax shrunken buck.

To fully understand, appreciate and accept the chemistry of a problem, consider the results when an important one can't be resolved. Being magnetic, a problem contains both negative and positive elements. These attract as well as repel. Most of us down on our luck begin to despair when we could be at the turning point and on the way up. Those who accept this analysis soon discover an almost magical way to control fear and inner turmoil. Learning to make contact with the power generated by a problem, and harnessing it to achieve a satisfactory solution, adds a new zest to living.

23

Consider each crisis as beneficial to the brain as exercise to the body. Recognize the simple fact that it takes some people a long time to reach their full potential while all too many never leave a teenage understanding of life. Should some be considered luckier than others? Does luck actually help them live a true life Horatio Alger success story? The author thinks not. He believes the difference lies in one's willingness to grow, to face and attempt to resolve whatever fate has placed within one's conscious and subconscious area of activity. To solve the greatest number frequently requires shelving a problem until needed advice can be found. Rather than seek an easy answer, or escape through drink, drugs, over indulgence in sex, food, etc., those destined for success reposition the problem on their Solution Schedule and allow time to help them find a satisfactory answer.

Consider the lives of those who substantiate this thought: Thomas Edison, Marconi, Madame Curie and countless others who made major constrictions. Each followed a formula that brought fame and fortune. The fabric of every forward step is woven with the same golden thread. Each summoned sufficient courage and perseverance to do something they had never done before. Without fully recognizing the end result, each lived comparable lives. Each used time to fulfill a dream. When you accept the fact that a minute today is worth an hour tomorrow, and invest each precious minute in constructive effort, you lend fate a helping hand.

To substantiate this concept, note the many strange ways others "strike it rich." A destitute miner hears a rumor and drops off a slow moving freight train in a wilderness area. Many months later he discovers a gold mine. Treasure hunters discover a sunken ship containing Spanish bullion because a navigator refused to allow a vicious storm to prevent reaching a previously scheduled exploration site. Because I couldn't afford to waste lumber selling at 4½¢ a square foot during the Great Depression, luck smiled when I applied the concept of a full size dress pattern to lumber. And so it goes, everyone is given great opportunities when they refocus their mentalens, the mind's eye, and harness the power in every problem.

As this book goes to press, the nation is fighting a Third World War no one has declared, admitted or publicized, yet a whole generation of its youth is being systematically wiped out by readily available drugs. The sanctity of marriage and religious belief in the family unit, the strength that built this nation, is being sabotaged by advocates of sex without a marriage vow. The nation's currency is being destroyed by inflation and extortionist taxation. Bureaucratic regulations encourage anarchy by municipal employees while government sponsored laws pay strikers to strike. The free enterprise system, the life blood of the world's greatest industrial power, is being drained by politicians who never worked in the free enterprise system; by excessive minimum wage rates, ever higher unemployment, welfare and strike benefits. The criminal element, the front line troops of every communist takeover, are protected, coddled and released to prey on and destroy a peace loving society. Everything possible is being done to lower productivity and create labor unrest. Management is no longer is control. Politicians who couldn't hold a job in industry now dictate and arbitrate terms of employment.

Qualified job applicants can no longer be hired if a misfit with no experience has also applied. Thousands of jobs are lost as industry closes plants where management is no longer allowed to manage and where employees sabotage the quality of the goods produced. Millions of true blooded Americans now find it imperative to shift their mental gears. Each realizes survival depends on their being a jack of all trades as in colonial times.

This was clearly illustrated in a letter from a shop foreman. While a long time, experienced, capable and loyal employee of a major company making parts for the auto industry, he began getting "temporary layoffs" all too frequently. As his unemployment benefits began running out, he started climbing the walls with worry. With time to think and observe, he realized the talk of a drug problem in the above average income school, attended by his two teenage daughters, was far more serious than he previously realized. Three of his neighbors' children were already hooked. His girls had one overwhelming interest — horses. To keep them interested, occupied and too busy to become joiners, he had encouraged their riding regularly. Now, without income, it had to stop. This created a need to find other activities or be vulnerable to their peers.

Living on three acres adjacent to a state park that contained miles of trails, he read Book #679 How to Build a Stable.

Book #679

Although he had never done much carpentry and had no construction experience, working his way up the ladder in the auto parts company helped develop mechanical skills. He read the book and, finding that every step from laying out guide lines for footings, to building a cupola, were clearly explained, he decided to find out what material might cost.

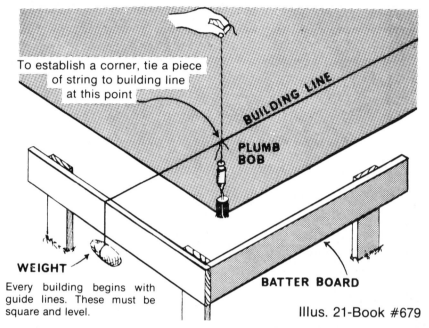

To establish a corner, tie a piece of string to building line at this point

BUILDING LINE

PLUMB BOB

WEIGHT

Every building begins with guide lines. These must be square and level.

BATTER BOARD

Illus. 21-Book #679

After a little shopping, he was agreeably surprised to learn its cost was between one half to two thirds less than what a contractor might charge. He next talked to the vice president of the bank holding the mortgage on his home. He explained layoffs at the plant provided ample time to build and if he were called back, he could still complete construction in his spare time. He estimated rent from three stalls would pay interest and help amortize the loan. The V.P., with three "horse crazy" daughters, was also concerned about the drug problem. He thought the idea both logical and timely and agreed, if he decided to build, to approve a loan. Since good stable facilities were in short supply, all agreed the question of finding acceptable boarders presented no problem. When the meeting broke up and the others left, the V.P. said, "The idea is more timely and logical from still another angle. One drug cure costs far more than material for a barn."

On finding the bank agreeable, he discussed the stable idea with his family. It created so much enthusiasm no one slept for the next three nights. Since finding boarders presented no probem, the question of chores, feeding,mucking out and grooming, was soon arranged. From the moment a decision to build was finalized, the transformation in the girl's use of time was absolute. No longer was either one dependent on a friend to do this or that. No longer was an invitation needed to have a good time. Every spare hour was invested in its construction. Shopping for material when same was needed, doing anything and everything they had never even imagined doing, helped create a unity the family had never previously experienced. Each developed maturity as they labored to make a dream come true. No task seemed too difficult. They helped lay out guide lines, dig trenches for the foundation, another for the water and electric line. As directions explained every step, they knew when to reach for a level, when to check with a plumb bob line.

The entire family gained on site experience in the construction trades. It also provided the father with nights of peaceful sleep. He was now converting time into a sizeable Capital Gain with only an investment of time and material. Building the barn absorbed the entire family's use of spare time for almost eight months. Before the foundation had been completed, word got around and six horse owners wanted to reserve stall space.

As the stable neared completion, the father was again called back to the plant. Where before he was satisfied, he now felt the work lacked any future. Construction continued over weekends and holidays. As visitors began to inspect the stable and appreciated how well it was planned, he was asked to build one for a vice president of a local corporation. Since business at the plant was still sluggish, he requested a temporary leave of absence which was willingly granted. Completion of the second building generated additional orders. Being a mason, carpenter and builder proved so satisfying he decided to resign from the plant. Six months after making this decision, the plant was shut down with no reopening date scheduled.

Transforming time into building labor saved a mind, created hope in the future, while it generated a sizeable Capital Gains. Creating a profitable use of every spare hour provided the stable with needed help while it insured two teenagers survival during a difficult time of life.

Illus. 4 - Book #679

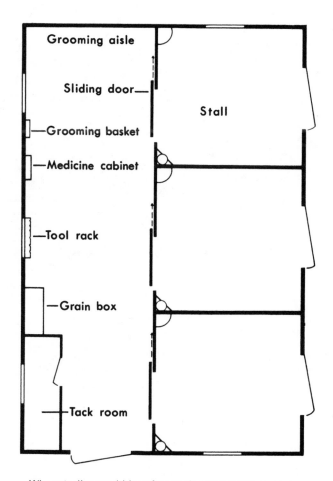

Where trails are within safe over the road distance, and size of property permits, a stable can add income plus a capital gains. It also increases property taxes.

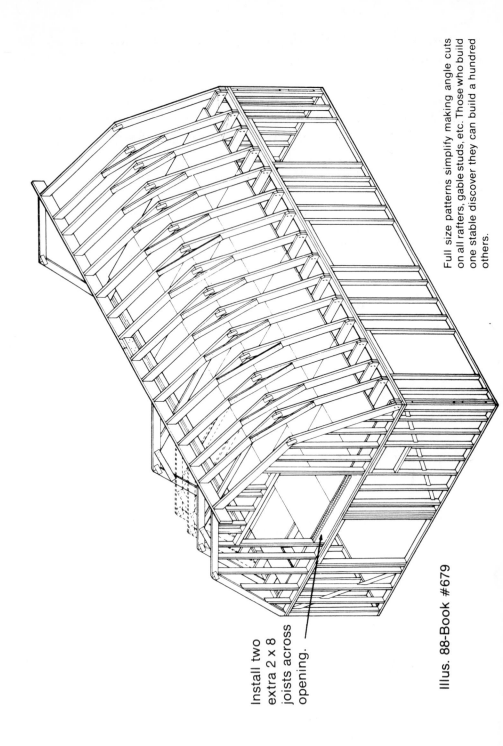

Install two
extra 2 x 8
joists across
opening.

Illus. 88-Book #679

Full size patterns simplify making angle cuts on all rafters, gable studs, etc. Those who build one stable discover they can build a hundred others.

Stall rental was sufficient to pay interest and amortization on the loan plus cover the additional property taxes.

Both girls began to live a way of life they had never previously dreamed possible. As both loved working with horses, every free minute was filled. Being permitted to exercise a horse when an owner couldn't ride gave them more riding than they previously could afford. Both became excellent riders and experienced horsewomen.

In this situation, the temporary layoffs and plant closing proved a blessing in disguise since it opened doors to an entirely new area of activity. It also emphasized how little we know of what we can actually do or the many elements that continually shape the future of those who TRY.

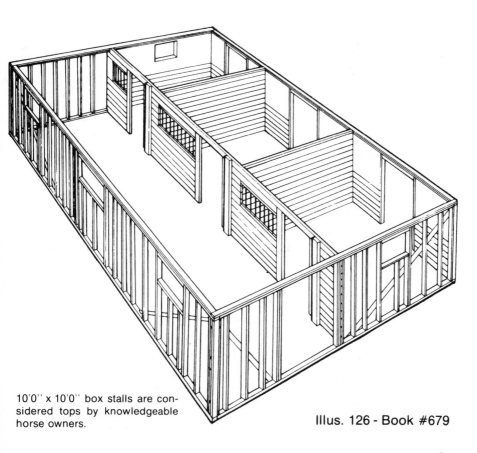

10'0'' x 10'0'' box stalls are considered tops by knowledgeable horse owners.

Illus. 126 - Book #679

31

One seemingly unrelated factor that materially affects the profitable operation of a stable when no employee problems are involved, stems from a little known fact, i.e., a good marriage provides the best man-woman relationship. This is basic to the growth and strength of every civilization. A poor marriage is a highly destructive force. As the divorce rate climbs and the marriage rate declines, more and more singles are creating short term relationships. Even more are going it alone. While a good marriage consumes a massive amount of time in making a home a better place to live, and helping one another meet life's daily problems, singles find "doing something" absolutely essential to maintaining their mental balance. Horse ownership and riding provide a time consuming interest, exercise and instant release from tension. The need to "keep going" has created a bonanza for stable owners even during past recessions. Today's stabling facilities charge and receive an all time high monthly board yet all who are interested gladly pay since a board bill is far less costly than visits to a psychiatrist.

According to a recent letter, "the unemployed auto plant worker" has built a total of eight three-box stall barns, one stretched out version containing twelve stalls, plus as many of the 8'0" x 10'0" red barn toolhouses as time permitted when he wasn't working on a larger project. He reported selling these to garden supply and home improvement centers as well as directly to homeowners. Buying material locally, building four wall and roof sections in his garage, then delivering same in a pickup truck, he effected sizeable savings. The sections are easily bolted together on the owner's foundation.

One vitally important suggestion: Don't start doing something you have never done before when you are tired. Always start with a clear mind and a willingness to make every step as directions suggest. Always stop the moment you become fatigued.

32

Toolhouse

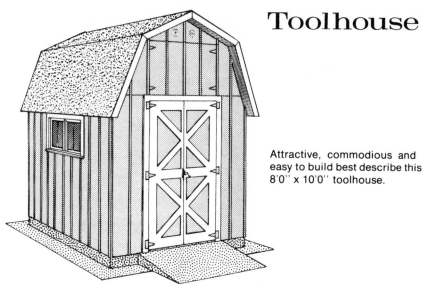

Attractive, commodious and easy to build best describe this 8'0" x 10'0" toolhouse.

Illus. 172,173 - Book #679

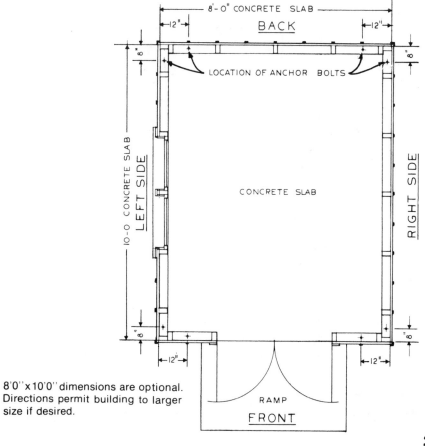

8'0" x 10'0" dimensions are optional. Directions permit building to larger size if desired.

33

TOOLHOUSE

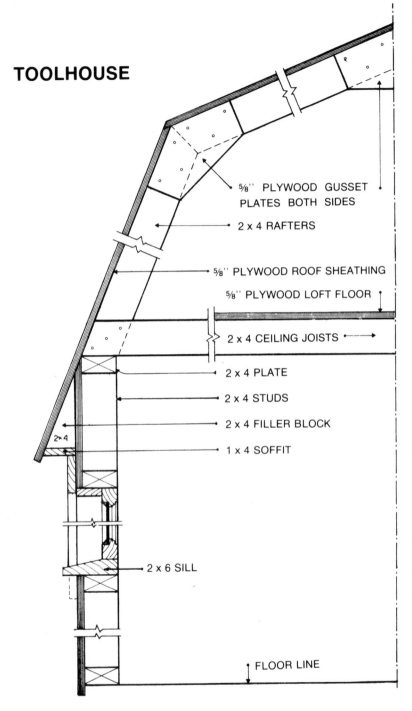

⅝'' PLYWOOD GUSSET PLATES BOTH SIDES

2 x 4 RAFTERS

⅝'' PLYWOOD ROOF SHEATHING

⅝'' PLYWOOD LOFT FLOOR

2 x 4 CEILING JOISTS

2 x 4 PLATE

2 x 4 STUDS

2 x 4 FILLER BLOCK

1 x 4 SOFFIT

2 x 4

2 x 6 SILL

FLOOR LINE

Illus. 188 - Book #679

Learning to build one builds self confidence. The potential for these toolhouses is unlimited.

A Red Barn House

How you relate to a problem, resolve or resist finding a solution, is what makes life so interesting. One management executive who read the stable book suddenly realized its size and appearance were just what she wanted in a weekend house. Having already purchased a piece of land well away from a rural community, she read and reread Book #679. On her next visit to the property, she stopped at a local lumber yard and asked them to quote on the cost of all material. She left a typed list of all framing material as offered in the book. On finding its cost far less than she had imagined, she asked the lumber yard manager if he happened to know of a local carpenter who was "looking for work." He recommended two. When she finally made contact with one, she showed the book and inquired whether he would contract the needed labor. She explained having made a commitment for all material. Having read Book #679 and #609, she was able to talk like a pro when discussing where she wanted to frame in double hung windows, the entry door, interior partitions, height of floor joists for a second floor loft, etc.

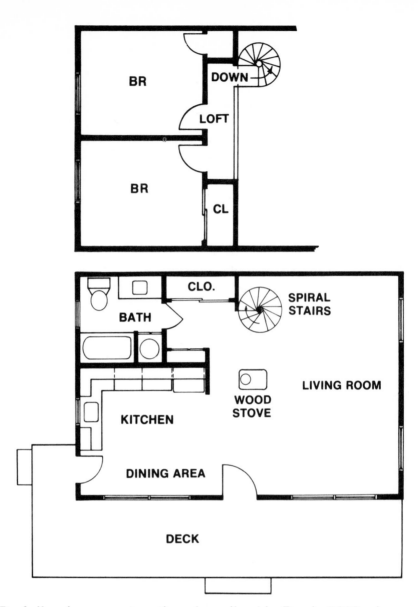

By following construction described in Book #609, she was able to plan partitions needed for a living room, kitchen, bathroom, plus one or two bedrooms in the loft. By requesting an estimate for all labor required to lay footings, foundation block, framing, roofing and interior partitions, she acted as her own contractor.

As it frequently happens, many pros don't think their customers know anything about construction. Both carpenters submitted highly inflated bids for labor. When the local vocational instructor heard about the job, he became interested and agreed to supervise four hours work each day using student labor. Each student would be paid a minimum hourly wage. With a vacation coming up, the executive agreed and supervised the first four weeks construction.

The lumberyard agreed to supply all material per original list as same was required. This helped eliminate loss through pilferage. She followed the same procedure when discussing the purchase of plumbing fixtures with a plumbing supply house. By following directions in Book #682 How to Add an Extra Bathroom and kitchen equipment as specified in Book #758 How to Modernize a Kitchen, Build Base and Wall Cabinets, she was again able to ascertain equipment costs prior to purchase. Since directions explained how to build base and wall cabinets, when to install a drop in sink, etc., she was again able to talk like a pro when discussing the installation of hot and cold water lines, a water heater, sink, refrigerator and range. Buying all equipment insured getting the quality she wanted without paying a premium to have someone buy it for her.

Not having to meet a deadline, and having fixed labor costs, she was able to shop for a licensed plumber and electrician as she had shopped for material. The plumbing supply house was happy to recommend plumbers looking for extra customers. The electrical distributor gladly recommended local electricians. With no previous experience as a builder or previous knowledge of material needed, she easily made the needed changes to transform the stable into a red barn country home. The savings in overall costs were substantial.

Since all material and equipment was paid for as purchased, the cash discount added a sizeable savings. A year after completion and occupancy, an urgent need to raise substantial cash necessitated taking out a mortgage. After having an appraisal made, a local bank agreed to a mortgage that exceeded all costs of construction by over five thousand dollars.

To Learn and Earn

Unless you go to a vocational school and study a trade, i.e., plumbing, carpentry, electrical, masonry, roofing, framing, etc., you find few ads in the Help Wanted columns advertising for a plumber's or electrician's assistant. Most skilled trades only accept apprentices when they believe they can find the needed work. In some fields, you need political pull to even get on the waiting list.

Since every housing unit, single or multiple family dwelling, has equipment that requires maintenance, repair or replacement, even those who can't read can learn a trade when they help someone who can. Helping a homeowner build an addition, transform a basement or garage into living space, turn unused space in an attic into a singles apartment with a skylight and outside stairs, takes time, labor and good direction. When you help, you learn. And what you learn on one job can attract similar jobs. You also benefit materially from the "sheep instinct." When one homeowner economically solves an important problem, many who see or hear about it are likely to do the same.

Every homeowner and tenant of a rental house must assume responsibility for the maintenance and repair of all fixtures and equipment. Everyone who buys a parcel of land and plans to build offers a golden opportunity to learn the building trades.

Lumber, hardware and book stores that sell Easi-Bild and similar type books create new job opportunities everytime a customer buys a book. As the economy forces everyone to make drastic adjustments, retirees and others living on fixed incomes must find additional sources of income.

Up to a few years ago, most zoning boards would not allow an owner of a house in an area zoned for single family occupancy to create separate living space. Recent Supreme Court Rulings have changed this. Where separate living space is needed for a relative, building an addition or transforming an attic, basement or garage presents no problem with one exception. All new construction, i.e., an addition or expanding a garage, must not go beyond an established distance from property line.

A retiree who attempts any of this modernization work needs physical help. He needs someone to carry lumber, paneling, etc. Ask every retailer who sells Easi-Bild books to help you help their customers. Ask them to place a POSITION WANTED card on or near the book rack. List your name, address and where you can be contacted if you don't have a phone. Be sure to add, "CHARACTER REFERENCES SUPPLIED."

When a prospective employer makes inquiry, find out what type of work they want you to do. Make a date convenient to them. If time allows, get a copy of the book. If you can't afford to buy it, borrow one from the public library. If you have difficulty reading, explain this during your first interview. Intelligent people welcome the opportunity to help those who need help, providing you pull your weight and do what needs to be done. The successful executive who built the red barn house and the shop foreman who built the red barn stables and toolhouses became employers of unskilled help. Each provided work within walking or bicycle distance of the job seekers home.

Ask your local lumber and hardware retailer to list your name on a POSITION WANTED bulletin board. This renders a real service to you, the community and himself. He builds goodwill for his customers while he cultivates yours. No one in search of work knows all the many places a job can materialize. A shakeup in top management affects some, while a plant closing requires drastic changes for others.

How people in every income level change their lifestyle and achieve success, fascinates those who desperately search to find their true potential. A letter from a high ranking executive of a large corporation described how the death of his invalid father necessitated finding safe living space for his aging mother. Since she had no desire to go into a nursing home and pay exhorbitant costs for mediocre care, his wife agreed the logical solution centered on building an addition as described in Book #609. Since this book was created to solve many different problems, i.e. add living space, income, provide an office at home for a doctor, lawyer, realtor, etc., directions tell how to build a 12 x 16 or 16 x 24' one or two story addition. Detailed assembly illustrations show exact location, length and size of each framing member. This simplifies extending wall frames to any length or width you wish to build.

One story addition with gable roof, cupola and outside entry door.

Illus. 1 - Book #609

40

Two story addition with outside entry door.   Illus. 5 - Book #609

Realizing the government confiscates a sizeable portion of every inheritance, the mother insisted on paying for all material, kitchen and bathroom fixtures and whatever plumbing, electrical and heating work was required. The addition provided the son and daughter-in-law with a babysitter when they wanted to go out, plus a feeling they were doing the right thing.

With the help of a neighbor's son and daughter, all work was done weekends, holidays and one vacation. By explaining exactly what each was to do, much of the work on footing trenches, footings and foundation was done by the two able bodied high school students desirous of earning extra money.

41

Floor plans recommend an outside entry. This insures as much privacy as possible. The first floor plan contains a living room, kitchen and dining area. The second floor contains two bedrooms and a bathroom. Other plans suggest installation of a bathroom on the first floor.

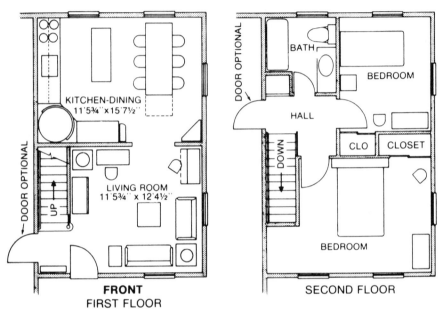

FRONT
FIRST FLOOR

SECOND FLOOR

Illus. 175,5 - Book #609

With taxes and rentals keeping pace with inflationary living costs, building an addition creates a tax deductible office at home. Help build one addition and many see, hear and become interested in your building the same for them.

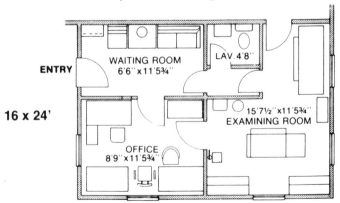

42

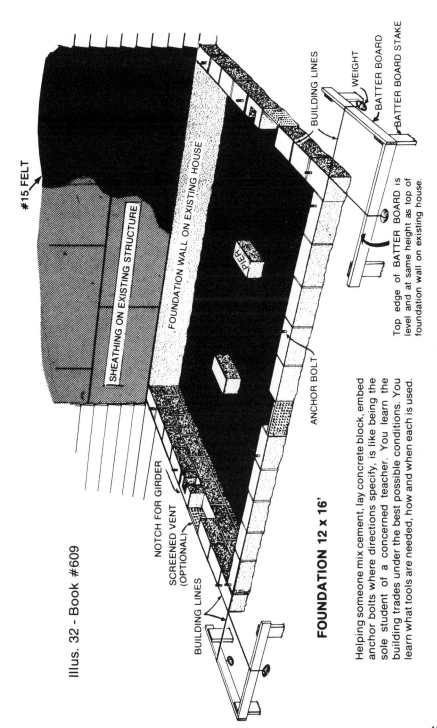

Illus. 32 - Book #609

#15 FELT

SHEATHING ON EXISTING STRUCTURE

FOUNDATION WALL ON EXISTING HOUSE

NOTCH FOR GIRDER

SCREENED VENT
(OPTIONAL)

BUILDING LINES

PIER

ANCHOR BOLT

BUILDING LINES

WEIGHT

BATTER BOARD

BATTER BOARD STAKE

Top edge of BATTER BOARD is
level and at same height as top of
foundation wall on existing house.

FOUNDATION 12 x 16'

Helping someone mix cement, lay concrete block, embed
anchor bolts where directions specify, is like being the
sole student of a concerned teacher. You learn the
building trades under the best possible conditions. You
learn what tools are needed, how and when each is used.

43

Books #675 Plumbing Repairs Simplified and #682 How to Install an Extra Bathroom explain roughing in supply and waste lines. Local codes require licensed plumbers to install all fixtures. Most existing hot air or hot water heating systems can be extended to serve the new space.

Few homeowners who wish to create extra living space know very much about building codes. When a code specifies, "All plumbing must meet local codes," they don't realize they still can rough in supply, waste and vent lines if they choose. Those who use vinyl plumbing, such as chlorinated polyvinyl chloride (CPVC or PVC) or polybutylene (PB), need only hand tools plus easy to apply solvent or cement. Easy to follow directions explain how to cut pipe to length required, apply solvent and all needed fittings.

Heat resistant polybutylene (PB) is a flexible pipe that is ideal for hot and cold water lines. You can also use CPVC for both hot and cold water lines. PB comes in ¼, ½, ¾ and 1'' inside diameter, in 25 and 100' coils, while CPVC is available in ½ and ¾'' diameter in 10' lengths. It cuts easily. To make a square cut, slide a piece of aluminum tubing or a coupling over end and position it where you want to make a cut.

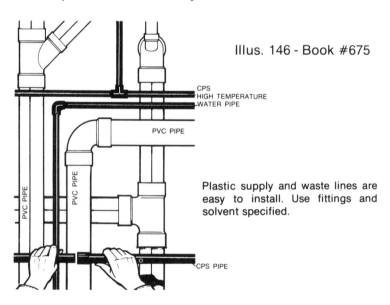

Illus. 146 - Book #675

CPS
HIGH TEMPERATURE
WATER PIPE

PVC PIPE

PVC PIPE

PVC PIPE

Plastic supply and waste lines are easy to install. Use fittings and solvent specified.

CPS PIPE

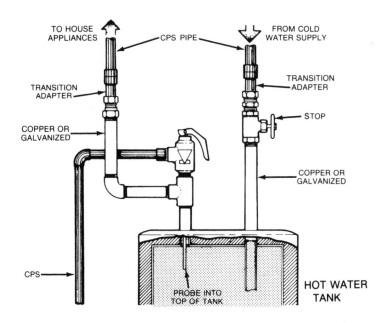

All fittings required for a complete bathroom and/or kitchen are available. Use the solvent or cement manufacturer specifies to weld the pipe to the fitting. The manufacturer also provides adapters that permit making a connection between a threaded metal supply line and the plastic. Every type of fitting is offered. These so simplify installation, amateurs soon feel like pros. Best of all, the image you create as a jack of all trades makes you feel a lot taller.

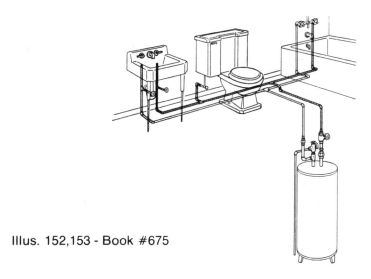

Illus. 152,153 - Book #675

45

How to Get Lucky

How someone hits a jackpot, solves a problem or finds a way of life they always dreamed of living is continually described in letters we receive from readers. Each reconfirms one essential fact: Regardless of past experience, age or sex, those willing to follow good direction reap a rich reward. An interesting sidelight to these letters were the contributing causes that required so many to "shift gears." Quite a few mentioned taking necessary action after their everyday lifestyle was torn asunder, i.e., loss of a job, a drinking problem, a plant closing or accident. What each accomplished produced results far beyond their expectations.

External forces such as inflation and high mortgage rates also created roadblocks that required others to find new job opportunities. One letter graphically told how the family had long dreamed of selling their present home because they always wanted a countrystyle kitchen with a fireplace or space for a woodburning stove. When housing costs and mortgage rates went through the roof, they realized they could no longer consider the plan. A friend told them about Book #609 How to Build an Addition which they had borrowed from the local library. On obtaining a copy, they realized it provided the answer. Instead of building the 16 x 24' addition, they did as directions suggested and framed in a stretched out version measuring 16'0" x 30'0". To maintain privacy, a front entry door was framed in the front wall as shown on page 42.

A son, recuperating after a drug cure, spent his spare time working on the project. After framing, sheathing and applying roofing as directions in Book #609 and 696 recommend, the connecting kitchen wall was opened up to extend the existing kitchen another 6'0". A prefabricated chimney and fireplace were set in this new wall following directions offered in Book #674.

46

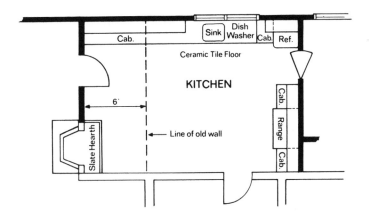

Prior to removing the outside wall, the ceiling joists were supported with a double 2x8 girder and two screw jacks.

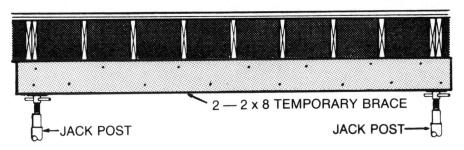

Installation of a permanent 2 x 12 girder and jack studs, as explained in Book #697, provided permanent support.

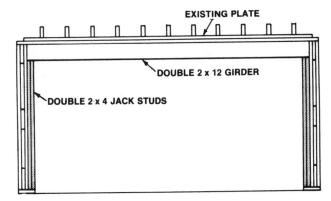

When the new wall was framed in, it not only added the six additional feet of living space, but also the fireplace. A door to the new addition was installed. The jack studs were concealed behind new base and wall cabinets.

By enclosing and insulating the fireplace and chimney, the family not only helped make a dream come true, but also gave all who participated on site experience in the building trades. The physical work and realization he could build shelter that added thousands of dollars to the value of the property gave the father a new outlook on life. On completion, he and the son went on to do the same work for others.

As fuel costs continue to climb, installation of a woodburning stove, or placing one in a fireplace offers an economic solution. Since every family faces rising living costs, it's an easy item to sell. In the installation mentioned above, the stove produced so much heat, the dining room door and entrance to the addition were kept open.

Woodburning stoves should be positioned on a quarry tile base or other equally fireproof material.

Hot water radiators in the new addition were connected to the existing furnace. Despite the addition of approximately 3840 cubic feet, total fuel costs were cut over 1/3 thanks to the continual operation of the woodburning stove.

The hours invested in building the addition proved a revelation to the entire family. As a top executive, constantly forced to make out of town trips, he had been under continual stress. To maintain the pace corporate politics required, he found relief drinking more than he should. Building the addition during every available spare hour provided complete release from tension. Nights were spent in peaceful sleep. Since the family also recognized the difference, it started him thinking about where he was going and what kind of life it would lead to. Since he enjoyed building and the physical effort made him feel years younger, he anazlyed his neighbors' and their friends' needs and realized he could help them save money.

Everyone who saw the kitchen and fireplace just about flipped. As many of their friends lived in houses with dated kitchens and a few already had more children than they planned, many needed more living space, extra bedrooms, etc. As he discussed "the space problem," he realized he had found a need and could fill it. His last letter contained an order and check for thirty one books. He wrote:

> "Thanks to your books, I have decided to go into the home improvement business. I have currently completed one job and have four who want the same. To give me help needed, my oldest son has decided to take a year off before going to college." With two sons now interested, he helped create a new business and a new life. A footnote mentioned, "One additional benefit, my blood pressure is back to normal, family relations couldn't be better, and Bless the Lord, no more commuting. Thanks again for those Easi-Bild Books."

Since insurance companies require a woodburning stove be placed on a non-flammable base, a quarry tile pad is a popular selling item. These should be made to overall size the stove manufacturer recommends. Use 6 x 6" quarry tile. Bond these to a ½ or ⅝" piece of plywood cut to overall size required, plus 2" in both directions. Use epoxy cement tile manufacturer recommends. Recess outside course ¾'' from edge of plywood. To cut plywood to exact size required, lay out and space tile ⅜'' apart.* Place molding along outside edge. Measure overall distance and cut plywood to size.

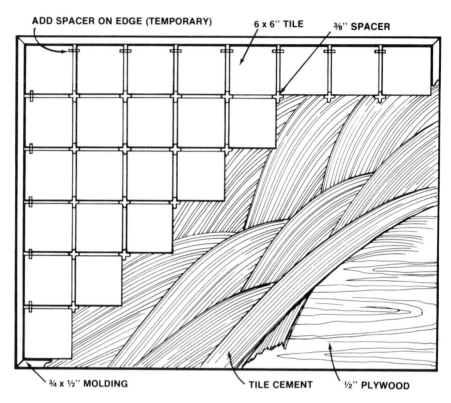

ADD SPACER ON EDGE (TEMPORARY)   6 x 6'' TILE   ⅜'' SPACER

¾ x ½'' MOLDING   TILE CEMENT   ½'' PLYWOOD

Your quarry tile retailer sells plastic spacers that permit laying tile as accurately as any pro. Most quarry tile manufacturers recommend a ⅜'' thick spacer. This permits grouting a ⅜'' joint as explained in detail in Book #606. Apply a strip of molding to outside edge after grouting.

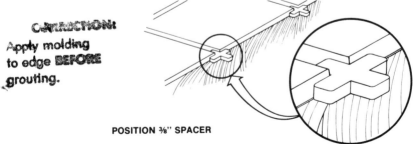

CORRECTION!
Apply molding
to edge BEFORE
grouting.

POSITION ⅜'' SPACER

* ¼'' spacers are available to provide a smaller joint.

50

Making and selling quarry tile mats for a woodburning stove has good market potential. All retailers who sell woodburning stoves should be contacted. Since a quarry tile pad is large and will weigh, depending on size, 60 to 100 or more pounds, buying them from a local source cuts costly shipping charges. Agree to deliver the pad to the customer to encourage more sales.

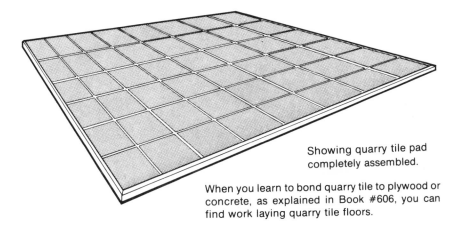

Showing quarry tile pad completely assembled.

When you learn to bond quarry tile to plywood or concrete, as explained in Book #606, you can find work laying quarry tile floors.

Those who go into business installing a fireplace or woodburning stove should become familiar with floor framing as shown in Books #674 and 697. Unless a floor is firm with no spring, no additional weight should be added until the joists below have been inspected and, where necessary, reinforced with bridging or gussets on one or both sides of a joist.

Illus. 86 - Book #674

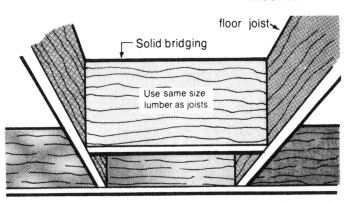

floor joist

Solid bridging

Use same size lumber as joists.

Be A Chimney Sweep

People admire anyone who can do what they fear to do. What people won't do for themselves creates business opportunity for those who can. As inflation and the cost of fuel oil necessitates saving money wherever possible, woodburning stoves and fireplaces are back in style.

Every home that has a stack of firewood is a logical prospect for a chimney cleaning job. Burning wood can provide big savings. It also builds an accumulation of soot, tar and creosote in both the flue lining and stovepipe. Unless this flammable accumulation is regularly removed, as most woodburning stove manufacturers recommend, it could start a hazardous chimney fire.

An adjustable flue cleaner now enables everyone willing to climb a ladder and work on a roof to start a part or full time chimney cleaning business. The flue cleaner is attached to a 30' length of chain. You will also need an aluminum extension ladder of sufficient length to place you alongside the top of the chimney or near the ridge, two or more large sheets of aluminum or hardboard of sufficient size to close each fireplace opening, a roll of 2" wide self sticking tape, the roofer's safety line and body harness shown on page 122, safety goggles, ankle high rubber soled sneakers, a hat and a large handkerchief or piece of clean material you can use to cover your nose and mouth.

An inexpensive chimney cleaner can be made using two burlap bags and old skid chains. Place one bag inside the other and load bag with some chains. Tie this to a long ⅜" nylon rope. The double thickness bag insulates chain. Never slam bag against lining of flue.

When you have gained experience, buy a set of chimney cleaning brushes and a suitable vacuum cleaner.

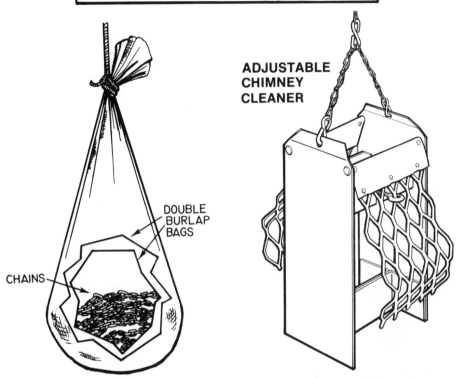

ADJUSTABLE CHIMNEY CLEANER

DOUBLE BURLAP BAGS

CHAINS

Prior to actual use of the cleaner, tie a handkerchief over your face to protect your nose and mouth, wear safety goggles and a hat. Wear no loose clothing and always use a body harness and a safety line as explained in Book #696.

Always place your ladder as close to the chimney as possible to eliminate taking any unnecessary steps on the roof.

To eliminate any complaint about damage to plants or shrubbery, ask owner for an OK when you have selected the best place to position the ladder.

NOTE: When placing a ladder on a flagstone or concrete walk or terrace, make certain you secure bottom with line to a stake or other fixed object.

When a prospective customer indicates interest, prior to doing any work, note whether the flashing around a chimney has opened up, the condition of roofing, etc. Note whether any overhanging branches have done any damage to the shingles. Point out any missing shingles or loose flashing to the owner. Loose flashing frequently causes leaks during a driving rain. If you are unable to see the flashing from the ground, be sure to notify the owner if you discover same at close inspection. It's important to call the owner's attention to these problems before you start to clean the chimney.

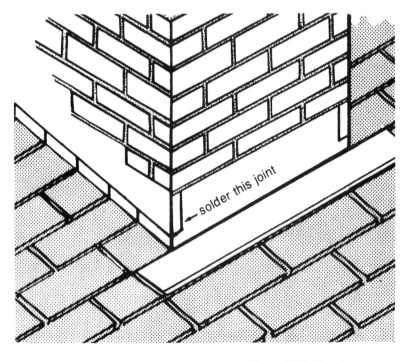

Illus. 257 - Book #674

Many pros prefer cleaning a warm chimney. If a fire is burned for 15 to 30 minutes in a fireplace, it warms the flue. This sets up a draft that carries dust and small particles up while loosening some of the built up soot. The heavy stuff will fall to the floor of the fireplace. Prior to cleaning a furnace flue, run the furnace for a like period. Make certain furnace is switched off before you start cleaning.

The actual work begins by removing your shoes and walking over the owner's prized living room carpeting. Spread a clean piece of polyethylene over the hearth and carpet and clean all ash out of the fireplace. Remove andirons.

Either open the fireplace flue or, better still, remove same. To make certain you will replace it in proper position, place a sticker on the bottom face near the left front edge. While many flues lift out, some may be frozen to the flue opener. In this case, open the flue as far as possible.

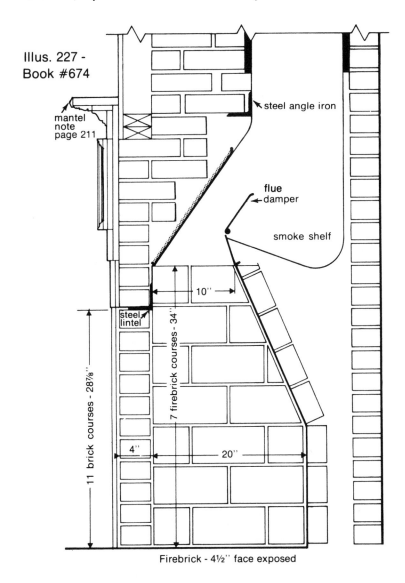

Illus. 227 -
Book #674

mantel note page 211

steel angle iron

flue damper

smoke shelf

10"

steel lintel

7 firebrick courses - 34"

11 brick courses - 28 7/8"

4"

20"

Firebrick - 4½" face exposed

55

Next cover the opening with a sufficiently large panel of aluminum, tin or hardboard so it can be taped across front and down both sides. Use 2'' wide self sticking tape to seal the bottom to the hearth. Use extreme care when sealing an opening so no soot or dust escapes.

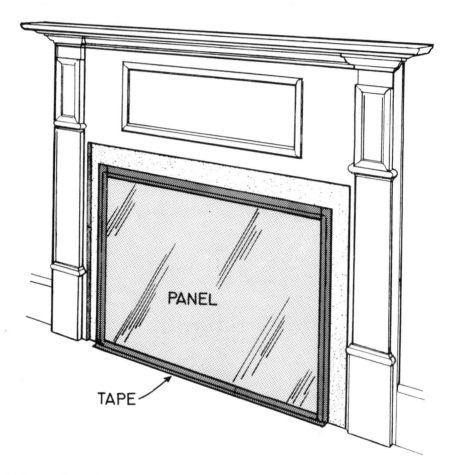

When cleaning a two or three faced fireplace opening, each face must be covered.

As each fireplace has a separate flue, and you may not know which flue is connected to which fireplace or furnace, it's important to cover each opening before climbing the ladder.

When you get up to the top of the chimney, you can easily ascertain the size and shape of the flue. Since some are round, square or rectangular, adjust the cleaner using the turnbuckle in the middle of the cleaner. This expands or contracts the cleaning wings from 7" to 12".

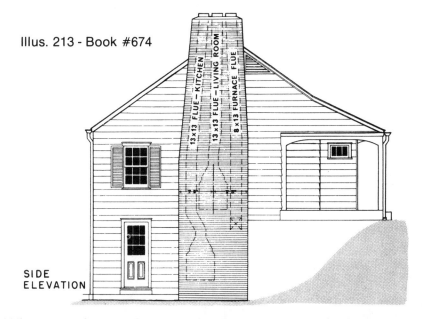

Illus. 213 - Book #674

SIDE ELEVATION

When starting each job, only clean a foot to two feet at a time. Work your way down. In a heavily sooted flue, you frequently find it's necessary to reset the cleaning arms to a wider width as it cleans away a heavy layer of soot. You do this by turning the turnbuckle. The turnbuckle permits cleaning an 8" to 12" round, or 7 x 12" rectangular flue. When cleaning a larger flue tile, clean one side, then the other.

Round chimneys frequently require ⅛" turns of the turnbuckle, up to four times to dislodge all soot.

After removing soot from the smoke shelf, floor of fireplace and/or from a cleanout door, disconnect and clean the stove pipe to the furnace or woodburning stove. Chimney fires start in the stovepipe.

If floor of fireplace doesn't have an ash chute, carefully scrape all soot into a container and remove same. Some ash pit cleanout doors are on the outside of the chimney, some are located in a basement.

If the fireplace has an ash dump in floor connected to a cleanout door, after all dust has been allowed to settle, remove cover and clean up soot.

If a fireplace opening is in a bright kitchen, you can frequently set a mirror on the floor at a slight angle so it reflects light up the chimney. This will tell you how well you cleaned the flue.

Replace flue and andirons.

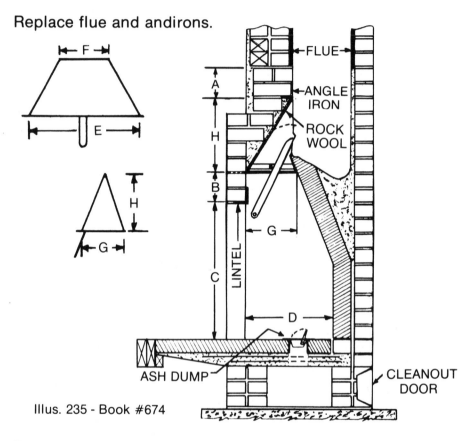

Illus. 235 - Book #674

Remember, woodburning stoves are great heat producers. Depending on the wood being burned, they also produce a lot of soot, tar, creosote and fly ash. It's not uncommon for some stoves to build up an inch layer of highly combustible substance on the flue lining in a matter of months. While no one relishes the idea of cleaning a chimney on a cold winter's day, it is important to allow the fire to go out, then take apart and clean the stovepipe connection. It's condition will alert you to the need for cleaning the entire flue.

58

NOTE: A chimney fire can generate temperatures rang-
ing from 2000 to 3000°. This expands metal parts and
cracks masonry. A chimney fire that burns only 15 to 20
minutes can frequently do extensive damage. Explain
these facts to every customer. Alert them to the need for a
periodic inspection if they decide to burn wood.

Where a masonry chimney is capped by a heavy piece of
flagstone, it's necessary to remove same before attempting
to clean. While some of these can be handled by one man,
where you face a heavy slate, it requires two.

Prior to removing, tie two 4 or 6' lengths of ½ or ⅜'' nylon in
position shown. Make a secure slip knot. Carefully remove
and rest it on the ridge. Tie it securely to the chimney while
the cleaning is in progress.

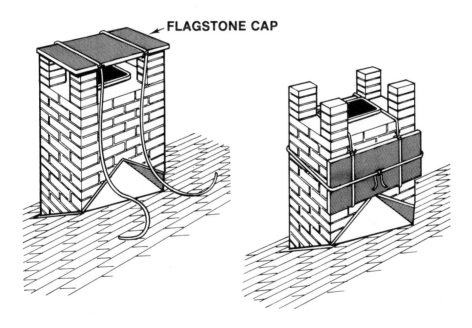

FLAGSTONE CAP

While many flagstone caps were originally leveled in position
with mortar, unless these reseat level, apply a little fresh
mortar to each corner when resetting.

If the flashing needs to be grouted or soldered, Book #674
provides complete details.

Many new retailers specializing in the sale of woodburning stoves welcome help in the installation of a prefabricated chimney. Read Book #674 and note how the pipe from the stove can go straight up through the house or through an outside wall.

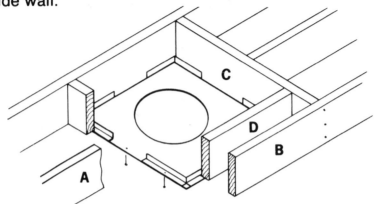

The prefabricated chimney installation, as explained in Book #674, can be made on the outside or through a second floor, attic and roof. Step-by-step directions specify size of opening required in a ceiling, how to frame to size, install fire stop spacers, insulated elbows, framing required for roof opening, etc.

Illus. 102,126,125 - Book #674

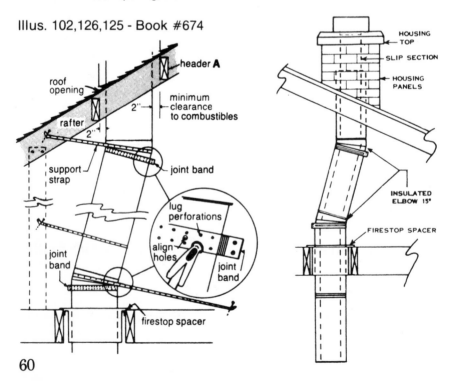

The trend to country style kitchens has created job opportunities for everyone who can lay ceramic and quarry tile. The new patterns of quarry tile and handsomely decorated ceramic tile appeal to all. Ceramic or quarry tile floors in kitchens and family rooms are fireproof, easy to clean and extremely decorative.

Read Book #606 and wherever possible make an installation. It's a great product to install. The new adhesives insure lifetime use, the customer is proud of the installation and when you do this work for one, you can do it for many others.

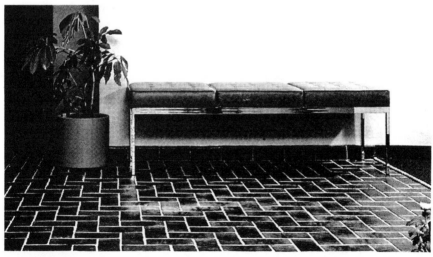

Book #606

As astute homeowners now recognize a home is today's soundest investment, they no longer hesitate to make needed improvements since each generates a Capital Gains.

Laying a ceramic or quarry tile floor in a garage or basement that is to be converted into living space, or in a countrystyle kitchen, not only simplifies housekeeping, but also increases its rental and sales value.

Thanks to tools that take all the mystery and most of the error out of cutting tile to exact size required, everyone can now make a professional installation. As Book #606 explains, a grease or china marker pencil permits drawing a line on the glazed surface. Using the handy ceramic tile cutter, score the tile along the drawn line with the wheel. Use a straight edge to keep the wheel on the line. Next center the cutter on the line, squeeze the handle and a clean break is made.

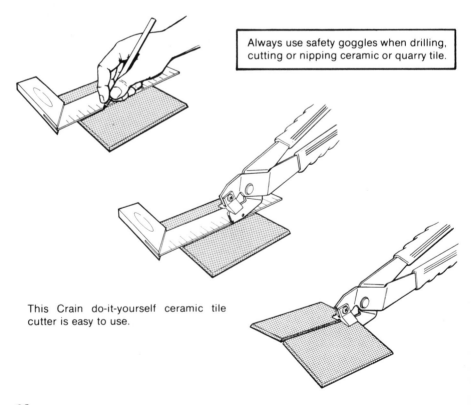

Always use safety goggles when drilling, cutting or nipping ceramic or quarry tile.

This Crain do-it-yourself ceramic tile cutter is easy to use.

Use carbide hole saw in ¼" drill.

Since faucets and shower heads require drilling a hole in ceramic tile, the new Crain tungsten carbide tipped hole saw turns amateurs into pros. This cuts a 1⅜" hole in the tile or on an edge. The ¼" masonry bit in center drills a hole that holds the cutter in place. A spring within the cutter ejects the piece cut out. This tool can be used on both ceramic and quarry tile. Since ceramic tile and tool rental stores have these tools available, those pressed for cash should rent the tools as soon as they get a job.

Almost every homeowner has loose or missing tile that needs replacing. Many have tile walls with joints that need regrouting. Making these repairs establishes a magnetic customer contact that invariably leads to other repairs and improvements

Center jaw nippers have carbide tipped cutting edges. Handle is spring activated.

One very concerned parent wrote to say she felt the hand of fate was really helping when she decided to remove the worn linoleum and lay a ceramic tile floor in their bathroom. Her husband started the job and pressured their sixteen year old school dropout son to help. While the father was a skilled mechanic, the son had little self confidence. On discovering he could drill holes and cut tile to exact size and shape required, he became fascinated with the idea of doing this work. When neighbors with the same linoleum problem were approached, he offered to do the work. One job led to

To remove hardened grout when making tile repairs, use this carbide grout saw.

This cutter will handle 4¼'' tiles diagonally or make straight cuts up to 6''. Also a big help to those laying quarry tile. Ask your ceramic tile or tool rental store about these cutters.

another and on his seventeenth birthday, he decided to go into business. He had letterheads and handbills printed. As a birthday gift, his smart parents gave him a complete set of ceramic and quarry tile tools.

As this young man and his parents learned, good direction helps create interest and confidence. Focusing one's mentalens on a skill one enjoys doing, and one others need and can afford to buy, helps insure survival and success.

Create Low Cost Living Space

Today's way of life has created a huge demand for safe housing. Singles and couples desperately search for a place where they can live in comparative safety. Retirees search for living space within the communities they lived as property owners.

Most elderly homeowning singles and couples desperately need more income. When you make the necessary connections, the power generated offers great opportunities.

Book #615

Book #603 How to Build a Dormer, #773 How to Create Room at the Top*, #665 How to Modernize an Attic, #615 How to Modernize a Basement, #684 How to Transform a Garage into Living Space, #763 How to Build a Two Car Garage with Apartment Above provide all the step-by-step direction.

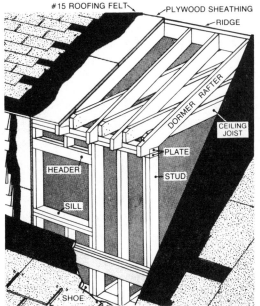

#15 ROOFING FELT · PLYWOOD SHEATHING · RIDGE · DORMER RAFTER · CEILING JOIST · PLATE · HEADER · STUD · SILL · SHOE

Illus. 1,26 - Book #773

Illustration indicates position of framing required for a dormer. Buy material as needed. You can reuse existing rafters or buy same size lumber. 2 x 6 ceiling joists can be used for unsupported spans up to ten feet; 2 x 8 for spans over ten feet. Use 2 x 4 for studs, plate, shoe and headers. Use ¾'' plywood for roof and side wall sheathing. Apply roofing shingles, siding, fascia and moldings to match those on house.

* Book #773 contains all the information offered in #603 and #665, plus vitally needed information.

67

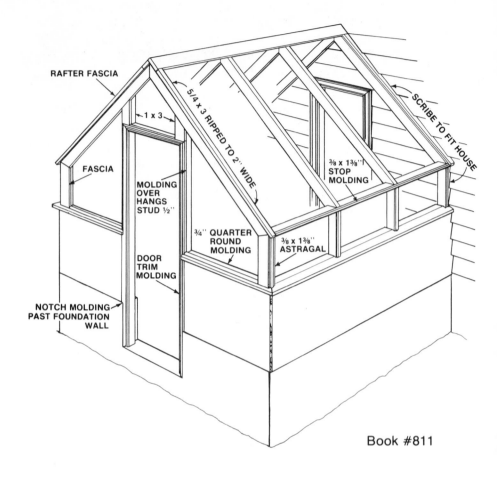

RAFTER FASCIA

5/4 x 3 RIPPED TO 2" WIDE

SCRIBE TO FIT HOUSE

1 x 3

FASCIA

MOLDING OVER HANGS STUD ½"

3/8 x 1 3/8" STOP MOLDING

¾" QUARTER ROUND MOLDING

3/8 x 1 3/8" ASTRAGAL

DOOR TRIM MOLDING

NOTCH MOLDING PAST FOUNDATION WALL

Book #811

As heating costs continue to rise, getting more square feet of living space out of every gallon of fuel oil helps insure economic survival. Every square foot that can be converted into living space also generates steady income. A basement containing a furnace provides heated living space when someone does something about it. Transforming it into a one room apartment with an outside entry isn't difficult. When offered to singles, they are happy to move into an apartment in a safe neighborhood. To get a 25 to 35% higher than average rent, build a walk-through greenhouse, as explained in Book #811. This acts as a vestibule while it provides the tenant with a time consuming hobby.

How you help one customer solve any problem is of prime interest to others. Learning to raise one or both sides of a roof with a dormer, build inside or outside stairs, install a skylight, transform an attic into an attractive apartment with a kitchenette and bathroom, is explained in Book #773.

The easiest and quickest way to get experience is to do what the book suggests. After you have converted one basement, attic or garage, use it as a sample. To attract customers, use a mailbox stuffer, an 8½ x 11'' sheet printed with this message:

WE CREATE
INCOME PRODUCING SPACE

We build additions,
transform garages, attics or basements
into income producing singles apartments

AT A COST YOU CAN AFFORD

Let us build a dormer,

inside or outside stairs
to a second floor apartment,

turn a garage
into a one room apartment,

add a second story apartment
to a two car garage.

We guarantee quality work.
References supplied.
We are insured home improvers.
Call us for a quote.

NAME
ADDRESS
TELEPHONE NO.

Illus. 4 - Book #684

As mortgage interest rates, material and labor costs remain at record high levels, and building sites become both scarce and costly, these conditions generate opportunity for all who seek work or want to start a business. House hungry singles now represent a big market. Working all day, they accept small space as the "in thing." It costs little to heat, no time to clean and offers safe living in good neighborhoods.

Zoning boards also recognize this new economic fact of life. All now recognize the safety and security of having another person living within close proximity of an elderly, taxpaying homeowner is in the best interest of the community.

Where additional living space, with privacy, is needed for an aging parent, divorced son or daughter, or other relative, many homeowners, and especially those living on fixed incomes, have discovered transforming a one car garage into a complete apartment, as explained in Book #684, provides a sensible, income producing and money saving solution to a housing problem. While the improvement will increase property taxes, it still provides an economically sound, income producing investment.

70

Since some one car garages do not provide sufficient head-room, directions explain how to jack up the existing structure, lay one or more courses of concrete block. It also explains how to extend overall length.

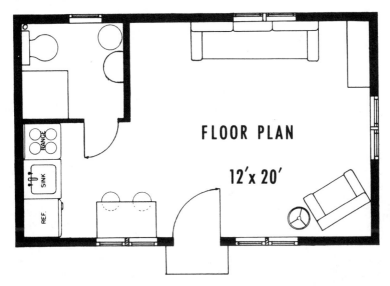

FLOOR PLAN

12' x 20'

As the floor plan indicates, the average garage provides sufficient space for a kitchenette and bathroom, plus a convert-a-bed sofa. Should the space prove too small, directions explain how to lengthen the garage.

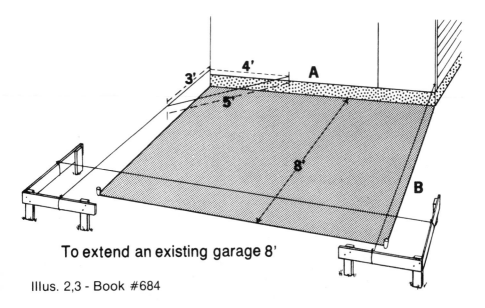

To extend an existing garage 8'

Illus. 2,3 - Book #684

As part of your presentation, explain the many other benefits besides income a "garage into shelter" offers. When people with mutual interests live in close proximity, both live in far greater safety. Police everywhere welcome help. An extra pair of eyes and ears can keep a better watch on who is doing what to whom. This shelter is especially popular with singles living alone. All too many living in high rise apartments become sitting ducks for a mugging, robbery or murder.

Because of rising crime, zoning boards now grant a permit where previously they opposed this kind of shelter in areas zoned for single family occupancy.

Tenants of these "one room houses" find heating costs can be kept to a minimum while they enjoy suburban living.

Two car two story garage   Illus. 1 - Book #763

Newlyweds, retirees and singles are prime prospects. Many find the two car garage, one and two story versions, as shown in Book #763, an ideal way to start marital life or economically live in retirement.

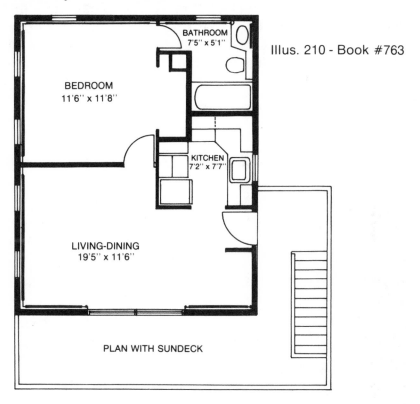

Illus. 210 - Book #763

BATHROOM
7'5" x 5'1"

BEDROOM
11'6" x 11'8"

KITCHEN
7'2" x 7'7"

LIVING-DINING
19'5" x 11'6"

PLAN WITH SUNDECK

Most people who have bought a building site are hesitant to borrow mortgage money at today's rates. They find the two story garage an economical first step. This provides shelter at the lowest possible cost in the shortest possible time. It also encourages their building a two, three or five bedroom house on the same site as explained on page 108.

When discussing this construction with an able bodied customer, suggest they help build it during their spare time. Offer to pay a minimum wage for each hour they invest.

If you decide to build to get experience and want to learn how a mason lays blocks, a plumber roughs in waste and supply lines, hire one who will allow you to help.

Working alongside an experienced electrician or plumber is like having a private tutor. Since Books #675 Plumbing Repairs Simplified, #682 How to Add an Extra Bathroom, #606 How to Lay Ceramic Tile, #605 How to Apply Paneling, etc., etc., explain HOW, reading through each book enables everyone interested to perform each step. Working alongside an experienced pro helps build self confidence while it soon confirms one important fact. Anyone can do anything if they follow good direction and make an effort.

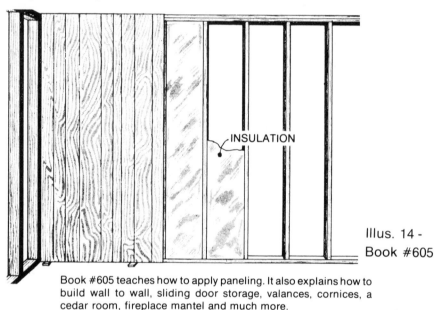

INSULATION

Illus. 14 -
Book #605

Book #605 teaches how to apply paneling. It also explains how to build wall to wall, sliding door storage, valances, cornices, a cedar room, fireplace mantel and much more.

At a recent housing convention, economists predicted the scarcity of useable building sites would materially change the living habits of the nation during the next ten years. They not only predicted single and two car garage apartments, but also the addition of a second story to an existing two car garage. This would provide one apartment on first floor, another on the second. Housing built to affordable size was the basic theme of most speakers.

Getting a piece of the action can begin by transforming the garage in your own backyard. On completion, invite prospective customers to see what can be done, how you can help them create more income, live in greater safety.

One young couple wrote to tell us their solution to finding low cost housing. Reading Books #609 How to Build an Addition and #685 How to Rehabilitate Abandoned Buildings encouraged them to purchase a piece of farmland at a tax sale. The only buildings on the site were a two story shell containing no wiring, plumbing or heat, plus an outhouse. Just after taking title, a high wind demolished the outhouse.

The floor joists under the first floor were badly eaten by termites. Since the house had no facilities, they considered tearing it down and starting from scratch. They called in a termite proofing service and the "expert" didn't even want to quote a figure. He advised tearing the "shack" down. His estimate would have to be more than what they had paid for the property.

Realizing they had nothing to lose, they decided to "termite proof" the premises following procedure explained on page 144. When they discovered this worked, they followed directions and added gusset beams to both sides of each joist, as explained in Book #684, then proceeded to build a 12 x 16' addition.

The structure now offered a 12 x 16' living room (the new addition), a dining room, kitchen and bathroom on the first floor, two bedrooms on the second floor.

Insulation was placed between ceiling joists over the new addition. This was covered with ⅝'' plywood flooring. A door into this "attic" provided an exceptional amount of storage space.

Realizing what they could do with one "shack" they could do with others, they invested the last five years buying, remodeling, renting or selling everything they could find "at a price," and having a ball doing the work. The effort not only paid off handsomely, but also created mutual respect that strengthened their marriage.

If you see any abandoned buildings, one, two, three or more stories high, located in the city, suburbs or farms, keep this transformation in mind. As the population ages, more and more people retire each year. Many yearn for the peace and quiet of country living.

Everytime anyone builds an addition, remodels a garage or kitchen, or performs any major home repair or improvement, they are potential employers of unskilled labor. When you see a lumber truck making a delivery, or any evidence of work in progress, stop and ask if they need any help.

Don't expect to get any easy work. Almost everyone welcomes help cleaning up, mixing concrete, hauling concrete block. Every job provides valuable on site job experience in the building trades.

The individual doing the work, your employer, may be like so many who never did it before. When they successfully complete the first job, they decide to start a business doing the same for others. You could find steady work and a new career within walking distance from where you live.

Get A Piece of the Big Money

Three economic and social factors now create unlimited opportunity for all who are willing to do what needs to be done.

. . . Living space is in short supply.

. . . Building costs are at record high levels.

. . . As the population expands and fewer people can afford the new houses being constructed, many from suburbia are moving back to the city and rehabilitating what were formerly abandoned buildings.

Every building that attracts this new lease on life represents a potential employer for those willing to work. Helping a new owner clean up debris, apply new wall board and paneling, flooring, paint and protect what he has rehabilitated, provides jobs for the unskilled, plus job training in the building trades. Everyone, and especially those who lack transportation, should watch for any activity that indicates someone is about to start a rehabilitation job.

If you want to get a head start, go to the library and ask for Book #685 How To Rehabilitate Abandoned Buildings. They may also have the same book under the same number entitled How To Remodel.

As with all Easi-Bild Books, #685 takes the reader from A — how to obtain a building, to B — cleaning up debris, boarding up windows, to Z — transforming four walls into highly acceptable living space. In easy to read direction, it explains how, when and where.

BEFORE

AFTER

Illus. 343 - Book #685

Every economic trend, up or down, creates opportunity for those who know what to look for. Singles, couples and families in need of shelter, but can't afford today's building costs or mortgage rates, find a once in a lifetime opportunity in the rehabilitation of an abandoned building. And what they see as opportunity creates work and a chance to gain experience in the building trades for those willing to help. Talk to each new owner. Offer to do any work they want done. Most prefer hiring someone who lives nearby.

Those who prefer being a landlord to being a tenant, discover Book #685 tells how to turn an abandoned store, one, two, three, four or five story walkup or warehouse, into income producing apartments. Most municipalities offer these abandoned buildings at whatever price they can get. Many were offered for as little as $1.00 to anyone who agreed to rehabilitate and occupy same. Since government funds are available for material and equipment needed to make this transformation; it offers equal opportunity to all.

A letter from one young reader reported getting considerable experience helping one owner. On completion of the first apartment, it was occupied by the owner. Work continued on the four other apartments. As each neared completion, they were immediately rented. A skeptical friend of the owner, seeing what he had done, decided to follow in his footsteps. By the time the last apartment had been rented, he had located a building and a second rehabilitation job had materialized. Renovation of this building took more than a year to complete. Both jobs proved more productive than time he had spent in school.

As the second building neared completion, and tenants wanted to rent, he began to think, if others can get a rehabilitation loan, why not him? Both employers willingly guided him through each step. While he had no capital to invest, they helped establish sufficient credentials so he could borrow a down payment. This enabled him to obtain a house that had been vacant for over 20 years and a rehabilitation loan.

80

BEFORE

Illus. 1,2 - Book #685   AFTER

81

Despite its location in a high crime area, as soon as the first floor apartment had been renovated, a tenant with two police dogs, trained as guard dogs, signed a lease. The tenant put up BEWARE OF DOGS signs and installed 10" alarm bells and floodlights on the front and back. Taking one dog with him when he went shopping and leaving the other at home permitted him to live in comparative safety. The new landlord moved upstairs and immediately started work on another apartment. As work on this apartment progressed, he had no trouble obtaining a tenant, and he again moved upstairs to maintain his occupancy agreement.

As he was no longer eligible for another rehabilitation loan, he continued doing rehabilitation work for others. The three buildings he had helped renovate attracted others who decided to do the same. As more and more people came into the neighborhood and wanted to remodel, he found it necessary to hire two helpers who desperately needed work. He recently wrote to say he now had five employees helping him with the work and in providing 24 hour protection to each tenant on a monthly fee.

Learning a trade, and using it to earn a living, enables one to help another. This graphically illustrates how the links in every chain of events help those who make an effort.

When it comes to the rehabilitation of abandoned buildings, the sheep instinct plays a major role. Only those with courage blaze any new trails. Once the trail is opened, others follow. When one building is made liveable, and tenants have learned to schedule their work and shopping during those hours when they can move in safety, the neighborhood begins to improve. Other families are attracted. Each makes the same effort and it doesn't take very long to resettle a neighborhood. As the neighborhood regains respectability, property values begin to move up and up. This isn't anything new. The pioneers of the old West lived dangerously to stake out and take title to a homestead. Today's pioneers are staking out valuable living space in the big cities. And, before long, it too will be in very short supply.

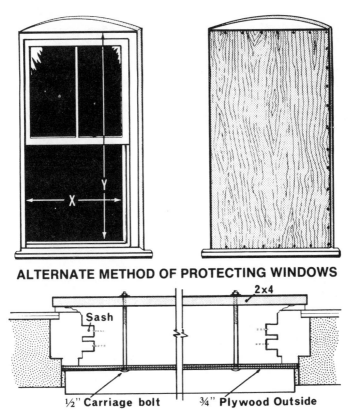

ALTERNATE METHOD OF PROTECTING WINDOWS

½" Carriage bolt   ¾" Plywood Outside

As Book #685 emphasizes, the first step in rehabilitating any building is to make it as intrusion proof and vandal proof as possible. Since most first floor windows will be out, don't use glass. Cover with plywood until you have completed interior renovation.

Illus. 3 - Book #685

Unlike their forefathers, today's pioneers have a rich uncle called Sam who is willing and able to underwrite the cost of the venture.

Only after all interior work is completed consider installation of window glass. In neighborhoods still being subjected to vandalism, use ⅛" acrylic in place of glass, then cover each window with practically shatterproof polycarbonate panels.

Double walled polycarbonate comes in 4 x 8' panels. These can be cut to size required with a saw having 10 to 14 teeth per inch, or you can order exact size required for each window. Besides protecting the window from breakage, the polycarbonate panel insulates the area and materially lowers fuel bills.

BEFORE

WHAT OTHERS CAN DO — YOU CAN DO

Illus. 344 -
Book #685

AFTER

BASEMENT —   Illus. 345 - Book #685

                                    — INTO APARTMENT

It's Worth A $60,000 Mortgage

Every city, regardless of size, contains unoccupied buildings. Owners pay taxes for as long as they think the property can be rented or sold. When unsuccessful, they stop paying and the municipality repossesses the property by default. Since these buildings are currently paying no taxes and depreciate each year at a faster rate than when occupied, the city fathers and government lending institutions finally decided to do something. New York is now turning abandoned buildings into co-ops. They offer each apartment at $250.00 providing the buyer agrees to renovate and occupy same.

Each building occupies a valuable piece of land, a full masonry basement, four walls and a roof. It represents a considerable value. As everyone who has had any contact with building soon discovers, the cost of excavating a basement, then building eight or nine foot masonry walls, buying the framing lumber required to build a one, two, three or four story building, costs a bundle. Buying these abandoned buildings gives everyone with guts a chance to mine gold. While some basements will need waterproofing, and many first floor joists and sills will need to be replaced, every step in renovation still provides more square feet of housing for the least amount of money.

All who seek work, low cost housing, income and/or a sizeable Capital Gains, can arrange financing through the Federal National Mortgage Association of 3900 Wisconsin Ave., NW, Washington, DC 20016. This agency provides a source for the funds needed. They don't make a loan directly to you. They agree to guarantee a local bank the money you need to rehabilitate the property. Here's how it works.

Let's take a typical case. This abandoned house (according to FANNIE MAE*) is worth possibly $63,200 when fully rehabilitated. A local lender, bank or savings and loan checks

86   *Federal National Mortgage Association

out the property and the individual seeking the loan. Backed by the government guarantee, the lender estimates the rehabilitated house as being worth $60,000. Under existing terms, the buyer of the house would be qualified for a 95%, 30 year conventional mortgage. Many of these houses are sold for $1.00 or whatever sum the municipality thinks they can get. The buyer also pays 5% or $3500.00. In return the bank arranges a $60,000 mortgage loan. $35,000 of this amount goes directly to the seller of the house (the municipality). The rest would be placed in an escrow account administered by the lender to help the buyer purchase needed material and equipment.

This program enables every able bodied, interested and ambitious individual to begin restoration immediately. Many camp out in the basement while restoring a first floor apartment. On completion, they move in or rent same and start work on a second floor.

Many single family residences in these once worn down neighborhoods have been converted into one and two room apartments. By screening applicants, considerable protection is provided singles living alone. The rental income more than pays interest and amortization on the mortgage, and taxes, while it provides living space for the owner.

Being a pioneer, one with the courage to carve out a way of life that makes you feel feet taller, is your choice. You can cop out with alcohol, drugs or crime, or you can live a way of life others only dream of living. Give yourself a chance to prove you can do it. If others can and are doing it, why not you?

A retiree writes:

"I have Book #685 which gave me the courage to purchase and renovate a 4 story walk-up. With the help of two strong unemployed youths, we cleaned debris out of two first floor rooms, moved in two dogs, two cats and a chemical toilet. We boarded up the windows exactly as suggested. We camped out for almost a year while we continually worked day and night. The work completely erased worries that had previously prevented me from getting a peaceful night's sleep. In looking back, I think it was one of the most exciting and fulfilling years of my life.

The dogs provided instant alerts and having a gun handy, I blasted away one night with blank shells, just to make sure whoever wanted to get in thought twice about trying. The cats kept the rats from bothering us. While I paid more than $1.00 for the building, when it's finally completed it will easily be worth a hundred and twenty five to one hundred and fifty thousand dollars. But we have no desire to sell. We have found a home and the rent money is more than paying for our living expenses, taxes and amortization on the rehabilitation loan. The people in the neighborhood come from every walk of life. They have accepted us and we them. The dogs and gun have established a certain standing that has, so far, worked out fine. We encountered all the hogwash most homeowners get everytime they need a big job done. One contractor quoted a cost of $13,325 just to replace first floor joists eaten away by termites, dry rot and fungus. Not having that kind of cash, I did it myself following your directions. I got the first book from the library, but would like to buy the following. Please rush #605, 606, 608, 615, 617, 674, 675, 682, 685, 694, 696 and 697. Thanks to your good books, the two boys and I are beginning to do almost everything that needs to be done.

Help Eliminate Fear

Harnessing fear is one of life's most important lessons. When a vicious crime has been committed, it creates new business for everyone seeking work. Offering to make windows and entry doors containing glass practically intrusion proof* by installing polycarbonate panels attracts many interested buyers.

Every type of window can be protected. For example, when converting a double hung window, cover the lower half with one panel, use a separate panel on the upper half.

Customers who want to open certain windows do this. Cover the upper half in two parts. Install an 8" wide panel across bottom half of upper window, cover the upper part with a panel cut to size required. In the summer, the 8" panel can be removed. This allows opening the lower window only 8".

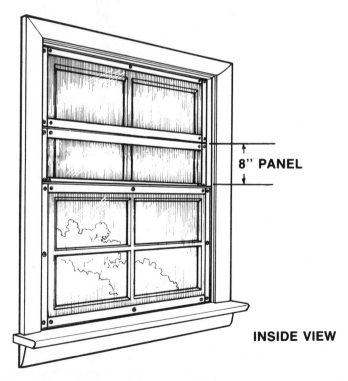

8" PANEL

INSIDE VIEW

*To prevent glass breakage by vandals, install panels on outside.

Applying polycarbonate panels, Thermo-Wall or equal to each window that could be entered by an intruder not only lessens fear of unwarranted intrusion but also cuts fuel bills. No longer does a large glass area lose valuable heat or allow cold to penetrate. The savings both in fuel and in peace of mind are substantial.

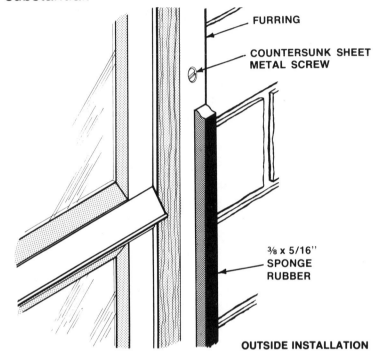

FURRING

COUNTERSUNK SHEET METAL SCREW

3/8 x 5/16"
SPONGE RUBBER

OUTSIDE INSTALLATION

Those who make one installation soon discover a whole new business can be developed when they contact school custodians, store, office and factory managers. All who are concerned with vandalism and/or high fuel heating costs are potential customers. While a school custodian can't place an order, he can be most helpful in recommending what you offer to those who make these decisions and in directing you to the individual at the Board of Education that can issue a purchase order. These orders run into hundreds, and in many cases, thousands of dollars. Every school, factory, warehouse, retailer or office building manager or owner is a prospect. Each type of window requires special handling. The homeowner who lives in a comparatively safe area finds the application of polycarbonate panels on the inside of all

90

windows a great way to make the window or door intrusion proof, plus a big fuel saver.

Schools and commercial buildings contain steel or aluminum awning type windows. These require protection from breakage. In this installation, it's first necessary to cut 1 x 2 or 5/4 x 2 down center. Always use furring (wood cut to size required) that positions polycarbonate ⅛ or ¼" beyond lippped edge of window. 5/4" lumber usually measures approximately 1-1/16" to 1⅛" thick.

In many cases, you will find placing a ⅜" wide, 5/16" thick, self adhesive, sponge rubber insulation tape over the furring helps seal a window better than fastening directly to the wood. This tape comes in two thicknesses, 3/16 and 5/16" and in 10' lengths.

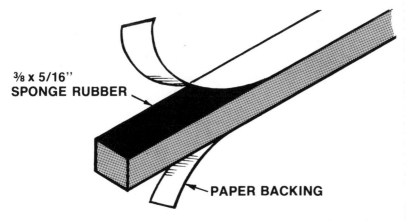

⅜ x 5/16" SPONGE RUBBER

PAPER BACKING

Cut wood strips to overall length frame requires. Place each strip in position. Paint wood with aluminum paint before fastening to frame. Using a steel bit, drill holes through wood, then into the steel or aluminum frame. Use sheet metal, self tapping screws to fasten furring to frame. Countersink heads. Apply sponge rubber to furring. Drill holes through polycarbonate and fasten to wood strips.

In areas where glass breakage is especially bad, go one step further. Staple #10 or #12 gauge vinyl to the furring before applying polycarbonate panels. A single thickness makes an excellent impact shield. A double thickness is even better.

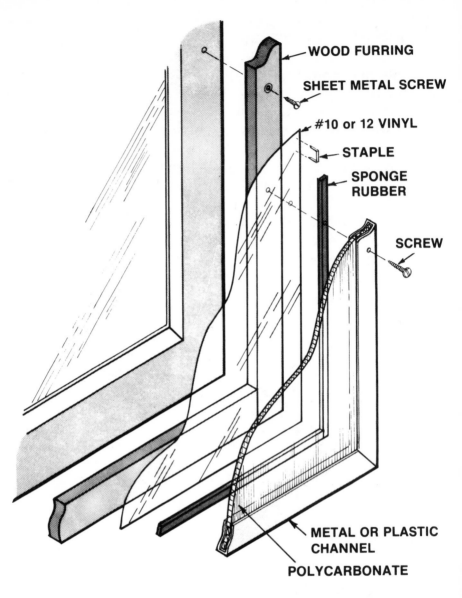

WOOD FURRING

SHEET METAL SCREW

#10 or 12 VINYL

STAPLE

SPONGE RUBBER

SCREW

METAL OR PLASTIC CHANNEL

POLYCARBONATE

Stretch vinyl to eliminate as much play as possible and staple every 6 to 8'' all the way around. It's important to stretch vinyl taut. Should a rock actually penetrate and shatter the double walled polycarbonate panel, and this isn't very likely, the vinyl still protects the glass. If an object should have sufficient force to break the Thermo-Wall and glass, the vinyl provides sufficient protection to keep rain out until a repair can be made.

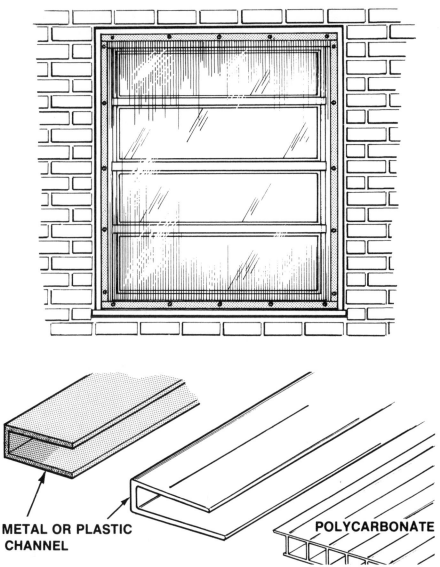

**METAL OR PLASTIC
CHANNEL**

POLYCARBONATE

After stapling vinyl to furring, apply plastic or aluminum U-channel to frame the polycarbonate panel. Drill holes through U-channel and polycarbonate one size larger than shank on screw. Covering all four edges with the plastic or aluminum U-channel makes a very professional installation.

When applying vinyl and Thermo-Wall, or just Thermo-Wall to a window with a wood frame, it can be screwed directly to outside frame.

Assemble a 12 x 12" sample of the 5/4" wood strips. Staple two thicknesses of vinyl. Only cover ⅔ of the frame with the second layer of vinyl. Screw polycarbonate panel over half the surface.

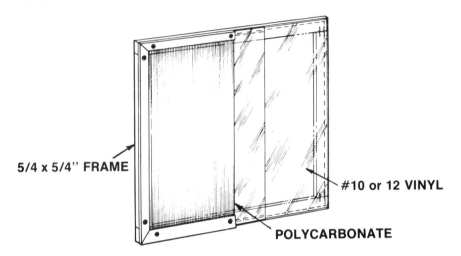

5/4 x 5/4" FRAME

#10 or 12 VINYL

POLYCARBONATE

When soliciting work at a school, factory, warehouse, professional or business office, retailer, etc., mention these facts:

To protect windows against breakage and/or break-ins, we recommend fastening ¾ x 1" or 5/4 x 1" furring to the outside face of each window. We then staple #10 or #12 gauge vinyl to the frame and apply 6mm Thermo-Wall to the furring. Any rock or object thrown with sufficient force to break the polycarbonate panel would still have to penetrate the vinyl. Even if the Thermo-Wall were damaged, and this would take more than a rock, the vinyl keeps out the elements until repairs can be made.

Always have samples of the #10 or #12 gauge vinyl. 6mm polycarbonate, plastic or aluminum U-channel available to show each customer. Thermo-Wall is available from glass and plastic distributors. If same isn't available locally, it can be shipped directly from distributor. Order exact size panel required for each window and same will be shipped cut to size specified. Write Thermo-Wall, P.O.Box 215, Briarcliff Manor, NY 10510, for price and delivery information. If you want to finish all edges with plastic U-channel, order lineal feet needed.

Double walled polycarbonate costs far more than glass. It is comparable in cost to 1/8 to 3/16" acrylic. Since it is shatter-proof and adds great insulation, it's well worth the added cost. While no acrylic, polycarbonate or vinyl can actually insure a building against intrusion or vandalism, it is by far the most effective deterrent, other than Mace, we have seen to date. Make a test. Try shattering a piece of 6mm twin walled polycarbonate with a rock that can be thrown any distance. Always show before and after samples to each prospective customer. Homeowners who live in neighborhoods subjected to rising crime find an investment in polycarbonate helps encourage more peaceful nights sleep.

Advise each prospective customer an installation on windows they don't plan on opening during the winter permits applying for an Energy Credit on Form 5695. This provides up to a $4000.00 tax deduction that may be used over a two year period. Homeowners should discuss this Energy Credit with those who prepare their income tax. Additional information is available by writing the Internal Revenue Bureau for Publication #903.

Form **5695**	**Energy Credits**			
Department of the Treasury Internal Revenue Service	▶ Attach to Form 1040. ▶ See Instructions on back.			

Name(s) as shown on Form 1040 — Your social security number

Enter in the space below the address of your principal residence on which the credit is claimed if it is different from the address shown on Form 1040.

Part I Fill in your energy conservation costs (but do not include repair or maintenance costs). If you have an unused energy credit carryover from the previous tax year and no energy savings costs this year, skip to Part III, line 20.

Was your principal residence substantially completed before April 20, 1977? . . . . ☐ Yes ☐ No
If you checked "No," do not fill in Part I.

1 Energy Conservation Items:		
a Insulation	1a	
b Storm (or thermal) windows or doors	1b	
c Caulking or weatherstripping	1c	
d Other items (list here)		
	1d	
	2	
	3	$2,000 00
ᵉ Form 5695, line 2 . . .	4	
	5	
	6	

Homeowners, realtors, professionals, shopkeepers, anyone who has glass in an entry door, should be approached. Making an application on the inside makes the door practically intrusion proof insofar as breaking a pane, reaching in and unlocking the door.

To fully appreciate the manner in which the mind accepts or rejects each thought and expenditure of effort, consider the electrical wiring concealed in the walls where you live. Switches control lighting, wall outlets supply power for every kind of appliance. Allow a loose or damaged wire, moisture, or other foreign matter bridge any two points of contact and it shorts the circuit. FEAR does the same to your thinking and energy producing capabilities, as easily as a drop of water can blow a fuse. To recognize and accept The Real You, and your potential, alert your conscious and subconscious thoughts to each action that generates fear.

Write the word FEAR on a pad of paper, then list each thought or action. Note the manner in which fear destroys your ability to think clearly, breathe normally, even enjoy sex. If you lose a job and few prospective ones are available, the list begins to build. It's at this point you must SHIFT YOUR MENTAL GEARS. Problems, like driving up a steep hill in a manual shift car, require shifting into second or first to compensate for the added load.

Fear is actually a fuse, a protective device, one that helps keep you alert, healthy and alive. When fear is allowed to short circuit your willingness to act, you begin to die long before you have learned to live. Expect to experience natural fear, i.e., a noise in the night, a walk down a dark, deserted street, being alone and ill. These are logical breeders of fear. Unless you instinctively react to protective fear, you could get killed a hundred times during a normal lifespan. The same percentage prevails when fear short circuits constructive effort. Until you find work you can do well, and take pride in doing, you can't expect full power from your mental circuit. The mind is actually like a spring loaded mechanism. It can drive you up hills to high hopes or down valleys to deep despair. The direction it takes depends on how you make contact with the power generated.

Like instant photography, learning to live is a skill everyone can master when they follow good direction. No one is born with all the talent required to meet life's many complicated problems. We are all conceived with genes containing some of the hopes, fears, dreams and ambitions of both parents.

Learning who you are, and what you can really accomplish, is no small task. And yet it's something everyone can begin to achieve when they analyze and accept the fact that the face they see in the mirror each morning is only one of many. What you see differs from what others see only moments later. The REAL YOU is constantly being shaped by conscious and subconscious vibrations emanating from people, places and inanimate objects. Learning to harness these vibrations helps dictate how long and how well we live.

Watch a photographer at work. Everytime the lens opening is adjusted to compensate for a different angle, light, shadow or distance, a new image appears. With all the skill a talented photographer possesses, he rarely produces a duplicate image when the angle, lighting or lens opening is altered. The many images he could take of the same person are but a few of those you see in the mirror morning after morning.

Every contact you make, every problem you face, every piece of good or bad luck generate positive and negative vibrations. These alter the image others see while it builds or destroys one's self confidence. Learning to build self respect, cultivating an ego that makes you feel good, requires facing each day and whatever the day offers without FEAR.

A popular and accepted belief among many, and particularly horseplayers, is that "they feel lucky". Research has long proven that people do become much luckier when they develop a talent called AWARENESS. These chosen people have learned to SEE, LISTEN, and COPE. They consider everyday problems as a car mechanic views any part that needs adjustment, lubrication or replacement. Rather than wait for it to become inoperative, they service it when there is a need.

Being AWARE is of special importance to youth, the job seeker, retiree and those about to retire. Learning to cope helps shape an individual. Allowing others to direct and dictate your destiny, destroys individual initiative. It also creates joiners. These are life's earliest losers. Joiners in today's society are quickly lost to drugs, alcohol and abnormal sex. Being an individual is vital to survival.

Individuals are unique people. Each develops a self sufficiency that enables them to think, act and make decisions that match most situations. This capability radiates positive vibrations which are greatly appreciated by those in need of intelligent guidance. Radiating a willingness to do whatever work is available, and conveying these feelings to those who can provide employment, is an important lesson to learn. Those in search of a job must expect to hear, "We don't have any work at present." This line of conversation has been practically dictated by government regulation. Today's experienced employer seldom hires without first checking references. And an intelligent employer seldom promises a job because they fear reprisal and a fine if they want to be selective and hire the most competent talent available. When you receive a rejection, ask permission to come back next week or month. Always make callbacks as often as permission is granted. Every callback provides a chance of getting better acquainted, of proving your sincerity and perseverance. Don't permit a rejection to discourage your effort. Remember, every contact provides valuable experience in learning what to, and what not to say.

Many employers, appreciating perseverance, make constructive suggestions that help you find work. Listen to everything said and thank them for offering their advice. Follow each recommendation before you attempt to see them again. Always report the results of any recommendation. This helps build the ego of those who offered same.

In making a cold turkey call on any business that looks busy, always inquire who is in charge of personnel. Always introduce yourself and give your name clearly. When an interview is granted, be sure to keep your eyes on those of the interviewer. Always answer the questions he or she asks. Don't volunteer information unless it refers to specialized experience pertinent to the job. All too many applicants, hungry for a job, talk too much. If the interviewer mentions "a job may be opening up in a few weeks," ask whether you may call back, whether they wish any more references as to your honesty, capability and willingness to work.

If they inquire, "What kind of work are you looking for," state you will take any job, at any salary the job pays. Making a favorable contact, even when no job is immediately available, is important. You have no way of knowing when one may materialize. Always express your thanks for the interview.

Learning to accept rejection is an important part of living. Making even one positive contact helps up your percentage. Since every life span is materially effected by your batting average, the more calls you make, the sooner you make a hit.

The nation's most sucessful entrepeneurs all lead similiar lives. Each took whatever job was available, at whatever salary the employer was willing to pay. Each spent years doing whatever work they could find, working alongside others from every social, ethnic and economic level. In retrospect, each considered these years a conditioning and hardening process. One that enabled them to find themselves, to accept rejection or success, while it tempered their ability to accept the many other disappointments everyone meets through much of their lives. While some make it big early in life, most don't begin to achieve any measure of success until their thirties, forties, fifties, sixties, and some, even in their seventies.

Sell A Needed Service

While looking for a job, consider creating one. If you live in a depressed area where crime is making life difficult for all who can't move out, create a service called protection. Offer to do any work where an alert pair of eyes and ears can be helpful. If industry has already fled the area, talk to store owners still trying to make it.

Visit your library and ask for Easi-Bild Book #695 How to Install Protective Alarm Devices. This book explains how to install every type of alarm. Read it through, then offer to install whatever safety device the customer can afford. These range from a piercing alarm bell, siren, floodlight, spotlight that can be activated without leaving the room, to more sophisticated electronic protective devices, i.e., magnetic contacts on each door and window, under carpet alarm devices, electronically controlled telephone dialer that alerts the police, to a single piece of 2 x 4 that prevents anyone from forcing a door open. When this safety bar is placed in position, it requires breaking a door off its hinges to gain entry.

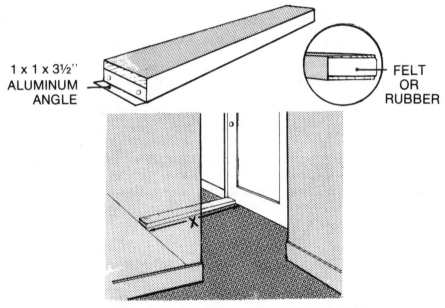

1 x 1 x 3½"
ALUMINUM
ANGLE

FELT
OR
RUBBER

Illus. 28,29 - Book #695

Today's unchecked crime is fast changing yesterday's life-styles. Where a short while ago, you could leave a front door unlocked, today most outside doors require more than one lock. Note the pattern of crime in your community. If a home, supermarket, service station, bank, pharmacy, liquor store or other business has reported a burglary, consider whether an alert civilian patrol could have prevented the crime. Ask concerned store and property owners whether they will help underwrite 24 hour surveilance. Many who experience difficulty sleeping through the night welcome something to do. Few know where or how to start. And no one should try it alone. Only start when two volunteers are available for each tour of duty. Don't attempt an arrest. Merely provide the eyes and ears needed to discourage a break-in. Visit police headquarters and explain the service you will be offering. Be prepared to notify the police whenever you sight strangers in an area where none should be.

Rising crime has created a boom in the installation of all kinds of protective alarm devices. The suggestions offered in Book #695 permit everyone, of any age, to start a part or full time business. Many protective devices are easy to install and while relatively inexpensive, work extremely well.

Sometime ago, we received a letter that stated:

> "I read your protective alarm book and found it most helpful during the time I installed an alarm system in my home. Since I am not finished, I need information where I can purchase the following." The letter listed those electronic components not readily available except by mail order. It went on to say, "I am probably one of your youngest readers. I am 16 years old and attend school."

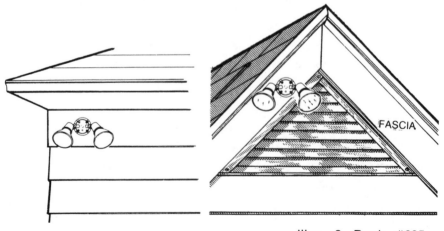

Illus. 3 - Book #695

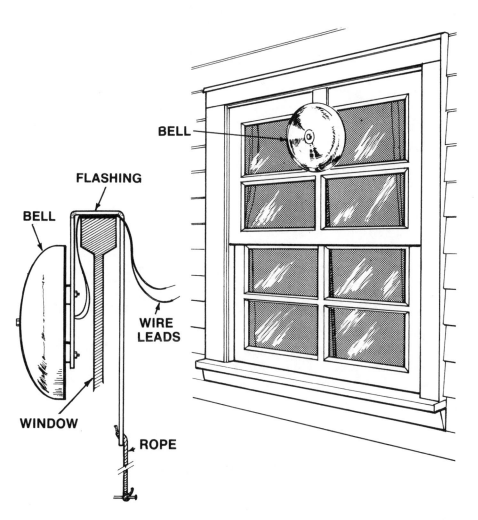

BELL

FLASHING

BELL

WIRE
LEADS

WINDOW

ROPE

Singles living alone, and all who live in an area where crime is on the rise, are receptive to any service that creates greater security. Many cutomers will want you to install an 8 or 10" alarm bell, and/or a 150 watt spotlight outside a bedroom window. When the light is focused on a window of a neighbor who has agreed to cooperate, both live in far more safety. If a landlord gives you a hard time about fastening a bell or floodlight in place, don't make a permanent installation. Buy a 1½ or 2" wide strip of aluminum or copper flashing, 18 to 24" in length. Drill a ¼" hole in each end. Bend it to fit over or under a window. Bolt the strip to the frame of the bell. Tie a piece of 1/8" nylon cord to the other end. Fasten this to a screw or nail.

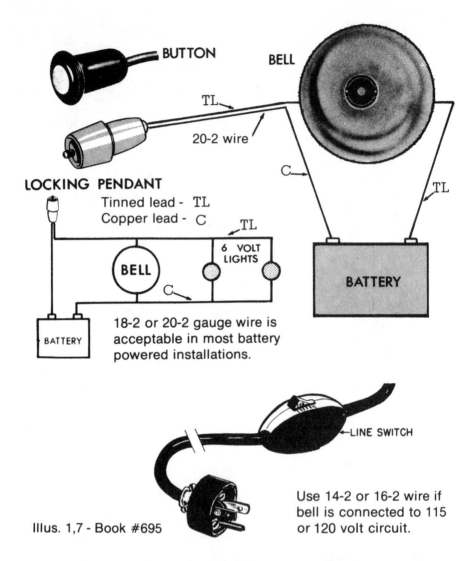

BUTTON

BELL

TL

20-2 wire

LOCKING PENDANT

Tinned lead - TL
Copper lead - C

TL

6 VOLT
LIGHTS

BELL

C

BATTERY

TL

C

TL

BATTERY

18-2 or 20-2 gauge wire is
acceptable in most battery
powered installations.

←LINE SWITCH

Illus. 1,7 - Book #695

Use 14-2 or 16-2 wire if
bell is connected to 115
or 120 volt circuit.

Connect the bell to a long extension cord as explained in Book #695. Place a line switch or push button, alongside the bed or wherever the customer requests same. Those who hear a strange noise or see anyone prowling can press the button. Criminals like peace and quiet. When an alarm bell outside a window sounds off, it unnerves the criminal as much as the intended victim is affected by a strange noise in the night. A criminal leaves a scene when he or she feels they have been detected.

Advise neighbors of each installation so they can take necessary action when an alarm sounds. Always fasten a line switch near the bed so it can be activated without leaving the room. This protection not only helps discourage a break-in but also lessens the fear of one. It's a simple and inexpensive way of helping everyone help themselves.

1 x 2

INSIDE VIEW

If a double hung window is selected, screw pieces of 1 x 2 in position shown. This permits opening window to height desired without permiting an intrusion.

Where several tenants in one building have engaged your services, set up a separate alarm bell code for each customer. For a client living on the first floor, recommend one long blast and instruct customer to count to five before pushing a second long blast. Always ask them to count to five between blasts. Two or three blasts on an 8 or 10" alarm bell and an intruder will attempt to escape fast.

A tenant living on a second floor would be advised to use two short blasts, count to ten, then two more short blasts. Apply the same code to each floor. This will help identify those who need help. Suggest installation of control switches in every room the customer requests. Use the necessary length of extension cord to position the control where it can easily be reached.

Sounding any kind of an alarm is a great determent. All too frequently the intended victim panics. Most crime succeeds because the victim freezes and becomes easy prey. The alarm helps instill instant courage. By triggering an alarm everyone knows something is wrong.

Always insist the customer test the bell after installation and to systematically test it at a given time when neighbors have been notified a test is being made. Its penetrating sound makes a deep impression and relieves much fear. Neighbors who don't make an installation still appreciate the protection it affords. When tenants take action, it discourages a break-in. Most criminals seek less alert working conditions.

To get a protective alarm or escort service started, offer it at whatever price customers can afford to pay. Be sure to include the name of as many local references (and their telephone number) as you can. If you know a minister, priest, rabbi, precinct police officer, druggist, grocer, etc., ask each if you may use their name as a reference. A week or two after you leave the first letter, follow up with a personal call. While few residents living in a high crime area will open their doors to a stranger, those in need will contact one of your references. When he or she substantiates your reliability, you begin to generate acceptance.

Offer to deliver goods to elderly people who fear leaving their room. Offer an escort service when they need to visit a doctor, dentist, etc. Everytime anyone is mugged, robbed or murdered, the victim not only suffers physical pain, but every business suffers an economic loss. Agreeing to deliver, or act as an escort, helps both the retailer and his customer. Every grocery, pharmacy and liquor store benefits from a service of this kind as will every person you contact. Always bear in mind many customers are living on welfare or very limited income. Few can afford any extra expense, but each seeks and needs the service you offer.

To get started, get a pad of paper and print your name, address and this message on each sheet, "I will run errands, help when you go shopping, walk a dog, or do any work you want done." Include local references and their telephone numbers. It's important for those who live alone to rely on someone they can trust. Since many won't have a telephone, suggest they slip a reply under the door when you return at a specified time. Insert your message in each mailbox or under the door of every apartment where an elderly person lives. Everyone benefits when shopping and living in an area is made as safe as possible.

As soon as you can afford to feed a dog, go to the nearest pound and find one that can be trained as a guard dog. Go to the library and get a book on guard dog training.

Offering protection fills an important need. While your initial fee will have to be small, learning to offer what others want to buy, and can afford, provides an intelligent exercise in learning to start a business. Remember, the more calls you make, the more retailers you talk to, dictates how soon you get your first customer. When you get one, others follow.

Create A Career

Just as a bee is born with, or develops a natural instinct that guides him to pollen, so must all who look for work develop an ability to search and sense opportunity. This capability isn't difficult to develop. It requires a willingness to follow good advice, then doing exactly as directions suggest. Consider these facts:

The national economy has long leaned on two basic industries, housing and automobiles. When the cost of labor, material and mortgage money went up, housing sales went down. This didn't lessen the need for housing. It did, in fact, increase demand for shelter people could afford.

When subversive elements took control of the auto industry and dictated what it would or would not do, it proved its power by producing a crop of lemons year after year. Smart buyers began buying imports and tens of thousands of employees faced temporary and permanent layoffs. Skilled mechanics in the auto industry seldom experience any difficulty finding work servicing cars, just as skilled building tradesmen found work in the repair and improvement field. The need for skilled craftsmen in both fields is now, and has always been, unlimited. Everyone willing and able to read can get into either the repair or improvement field or in creating new housing, and enjoy a lifetime of satisfying work.

Many begin a whole new life by transforming an existing garage into living space (#684), building and renting an addition (#609), building a two car garage with an apartment above (#763), while others invariably find a building site someone wants to sell. Creating a career provides an adventure in living. It offers a fun way to invest spare time.

One area relatively few fully appreciate exists among those who build a one, two or three bedroom house. They invest all their time in its construction. On completion, they rent or sell, then start the next one. Since most auto industry employees draw unemployment benefits for a specified period, they have living expenses during the construction of the first house. Those who currently own a house find little difficulty obtaining funds needed to buy material.

Singles, young couples and retirees are doing today what every able bodied citizen did during Colonial times. But nowadays they are building smaller houses and getting a lot more mileage out of every hour invested. They discover one simple fact: If they can saw one board, or drive one nail, they can drive a thousand.

All through the fifties and sixties slightly over 10% of the total number of houses constructed each year (over one hundred thousand annually) were built by individuals in their spare time. During the seventies, this percentage rose even higher. Each virgin builder accepted one idea, to wit, what others could do, so could they.

A 1950 Reader's Digest story entitled, Build a Home in Your Spare Time, Why Not?, told how people of all ages and economic backgrounds had built or were building a two bedroom ranch style house working from an Easi-Bild Pattern. Each invested weekends, holidays, vacation and "laid off" time. As the article reported, none had ever built a house previously, and few believed themselves capable of doing it.

Two Bedroom House Pattern #910

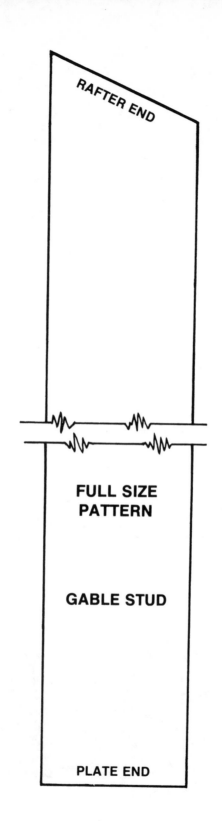

The author introduced the pattern method of building a house in 1946. It proved a unique building tool for two basic reasons. It enabled everyone who could read to build a house. It also took all the fear out of doing what needed to be done.

The pattern method assumed the reader had never built a house and explained each step in non-technical words and pictures. It proved so successful it encouraged thousands to build. Besides easy to read directions, it contained a complete material list that specified what to buy, where and when each piece of lumber was used. Full size patterns were included to simplify making exact angle cuts where required. The motivating idea incorporated into each pattern was to eliminate all fear and mystery.

Previous to the introduction of the pattern method of construction, the concept of investing spare time into building a house had never been fully exploited. During those years, most salaried employees worked five and a half days a week and received a two week vacation. Few realized that an investment of spare time could pay such a rich reward.

The first house pattern, a country cottage, appeared in the 1946 issue of the Woman's Home Companion. It was offered as a solution to a returning veteran's need to find low cost housing. It contained a living-bedroom with a convert-a-bed, a kitchenette and bathroom.

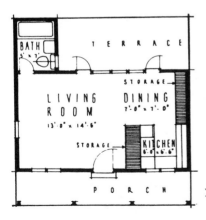

Pattern #91

111

The one time story pulled over ten thousand requests. It also produced an avalanche of letters requesting the information each needed so they could expand the house.

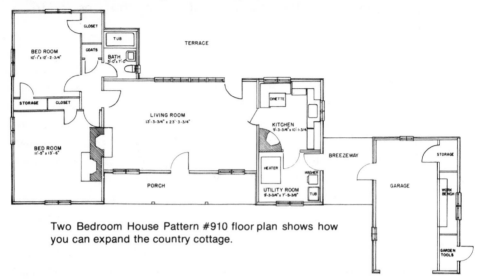

Two Bedroom House Pattern #910 floor plan shows how you can expand the country cottage.

To satisfy this demand, in 1947 Easi-Bild published complete directions that explained how to build a two bedroom ranch. This was Pattern #910. Those who had already built #91 could now work weekends adding two bedrooms, each with two closets, to one end of the original cottage, a full size kitchen, breezeway and garage. The response was so gratifying the author began to develop a whole assortment of house patterns.

In every letter received, and in each house we had an opportunity to visit, two elements seemed constant. The owner-builder had had no previous building experience. All had hired unskilled labor that wanted work. When it came to plumbing, wiring and heating, all had followed local codes and hired those licensed to do the work. The majority of those who built the initial houses discovered they liked doing it and found it a relaxing way to earn a living.

From the very beginning of the house pattern program, letters indicated many spare time builders were moving into their homes within eight, ten to twelve months time. While much of the interior work still needed to be done, i.e., insulating, paneling, building cabinets, installing ceilings, etc., all had built a house for much, much less than half current prices.

In the early fifties, five of the nation's leading house architects were asked to create three and five bedroom house plans for another national magazine. We developed patterns on the more popular designs. Each contained detailed directions an unskilled person could easily follow.

#501 Three Bedroom Ranch House, designed by Edward D. Stone. Its construction has been designed so it can be built any additional length by extending frames any number of 4 ft. units required. Fixed glass, window and door sections are interchangeable.

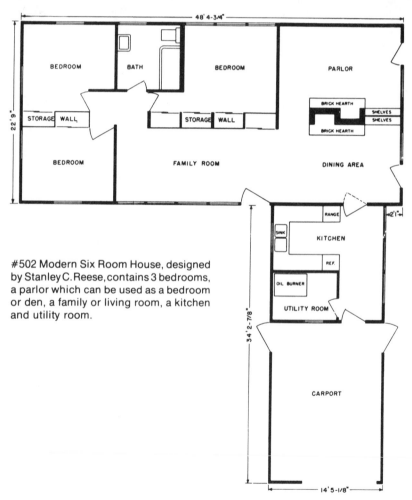

#502 Modern Six Room House, designed by Stanley C. Reese, contains 3 bedrooms, a parlor which can be used as a bedroom or den, a family or living room, a kitchen and utility room.

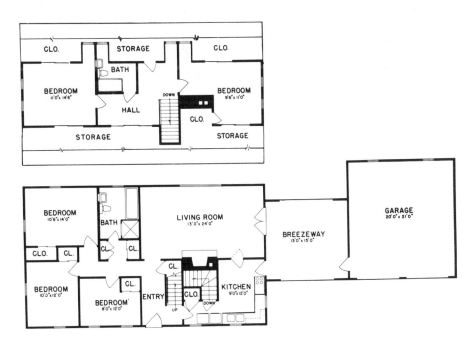

#514 Five Bedroom Cape Cod House, designed by Royal Barry Wills. This well styled home can accommodate a large family.

Today, more and more retirees are discovering the house they worked a lifetime to pay for is too big for their needs and too costly to heat. They seek "small houses." Book #632 How to Build a Vacation or Retirement House was created to fill this need.

Through the years, the pattern method of house construction helped shape the lives of thousands. While originally designed to appeal to an individual in search of a new career, it also appealed to group endeavors. Regardless of age, income or social position, many would volunteer to build a house for some member of the family, their minister, an injured police or fireman, or disabled veteran. In numerous areas, parishioners joined in building a house a year. This would be auctioned off to the highest bidder. Funds received would pay for material and profits would go to the church. It not only provided fund raising with no out of pocket expense, but also gave all who participated a quality of companionship they had never previously experienced.

116

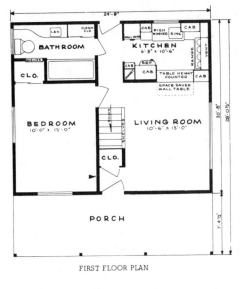

FIRST FLOOR PLAN

House built from directions offered in Book #632 can be constructed on a slab or over a full basement.

BASEMENT FLOOR PLAN

As floor plan indicates, this house offers many options. It can provide one to three bedrooms, a playroom, a truly magical kitchen, complete with a pass-through and dining counter; living room and bathroom. Directions explain how to build a one story and full basement.

According to recent studies, just under 11% of all houses constructed during 1976, 1977 and 1978 were built by individuals for their own occupancy. And this percentage seems to be in for a sizeable increase as more and more laid off workers get lengthy unemployment benefits.

The nation has always had a "housing problem." And people have always wanted to solve their housing problem at a cost they could afford. To get into the act, keep your eyes open. Anytime you see a foundation being started, a bulldozer excavating, a pile of 2 x 4's, inquire who is in charge and ask if they need any help. No matter what you earn in the beginning, it could be the start of a great career.

117

Learning to present what you have to offer, to those willing and able to buy, is the nuts and bolts of earning a living. Since everyone has problems, and solving each at a cost they can afford is what makes living worthwhile, people prefer buying to being sold.

How you relate to people is vital to your growth, happiness and longevity. If you happen to be one who "wants to do his own thing," wear a full beard or long hair, don't expect immediate acceptance from those who shave daily and cut their hair short. Regardless of how much you might help, the beginning of every relationship must stem from positive, not negative vibrations. Why try to overcome negative, inborn instincts when it's hard enough getting along? At one time or another we learn people are creatures of habit and environment. They feel alienated toward those who differ from their accepted standards.

The easiest way to start any business is to talk to as many prospective customers as possible. If you can't see them in person, do it by "advertising" your services. Use a flyer, a sheet of paper. Place it under a door or in a mailbox. When you have found and satisfied one customer at a cost they can afford, the contact provides a key. Keep the contact alive. Everyone they know and the retailers they patronize will begin to hear about your service. People who live comparable lives usually have comparable needs. A satisfied customer is your most valuable asset.

A business of your own can be started if you have a place to live and food to eat. Where you have no cash for material needed to do a job, tell your customer how much it costs. Many will buy the material to help get you started.

Your destiny is determined by how you use time. Sit on your butt at a bar, or before a TV and endless hours of God's inheritance go down the drain. Invest the same amount of time doing something you have never done before and living takes on a new meaning.

118

Many homeowners have had considerable experience and, in many cases, are equal to a pro in making repairs and improvements, while many more are still being taken by fast buck operators. Like nomads following the damage caused by a high wind, these operators move into every devastated area and quote whatever cost they think the customer is willing to pay. Since insurance or government funds are frequently available for repairs, home improvers frequently converge like a swarm of locusts.

All who want a career in the home repair and improvement field should know how these operators work. They advertise extensively over radio, TV and with flyers. Whenever a likely prospect responds to a roofing repair, kitchen modernization, two car garage or equal big ticket purchase, they call for an appointment. On arrival they note the neighborhood, condition of the house, its approximate value, the value of the cars they see parked in a driveway. All this before ringing the doorbell. When they get inside, they appraise the quality of furniture, kitchen equipment and appliances, even the clothes or value of any jewelry you may be wearing. Regardless of what repair or improvement is the reason for the call, their first consideration is to ascertain how little the owner knows about what needs to be done. They then price the work on what they think the traffic will bear. If the customer seems surprised or shocked, they invariably add, "It will take so many men X number of days to do the quality of work you want done."

When a large area has been hit with a high wind or flood, they apply pressure. They prepare a contract that states what work will be done and its cost. If you sign, you frequently wait weeks before they even begin to do the job, and when they do, you discover it takes half the number of men, half the time quoted, and they invariably do a mediocre job. When questioned about the difference in time and number of men, the usual response is, "We were lucky in getting our most capable men to do your job."

119

If the customer is a trusting soul, the salesman replies, "We really don't know how much damage has occurred until we actually start the job." Even astute businessmen frequently buy this "pig in a poke." They sign a contract that in no small sense grants a license to steal. The fast buck operator preys on the unwary. When they hook a "live one," the work proceeds at a leisurely pace by men who are experts in goofing off.

Many customers can smell this type of character so it's vitally important to create customer confidence in what you can and will do. Level with a customer who wants a kitchen modernization job done. Explain the facts, i.e., only after existing cabinets are ripped out will you see the condition of the flooring and joists below. Wherever possible go into a basement and test floor joists to ascertain whether they need replacement or reinforcing. Note whether existing flooring has any "spring." All this work takes time that can't be estimated unless you give yourself plenty of leeway.

The same straight talking approach should be used when you sell a ceramic tile floor or wall job. Until you actually remove existing floor covering, you won't know what condition the flooring is in. While a house with a full basement can greatly simplify inspection of floor joists and sub-flooring, in many cases you have to apply ⅜, ½ or ⅝" exterior grade plywood to entire floor to cover a badly worn area.

If you are discussing a roof repair or complete new roofing job, submitting an estimate prior to actually removing existing shingles can prove very risky. You may not only have to replace part of the roof sheathing, but also replace flashing. Always explain the many areas that must be inspected, and where necessary, repaired or replaced. Since a reroofing job starts by removing several courses of shingles, you can never tell what condition the sheathing is in until you see it. Suggest to each customer they have a lawyer or friend go over your proposed "work contract." Base this on a per item

120

basis. If the roof sheathing needs patching or replacing, alerting your customer to the added costs won't come as a surprise. This approach and procedure enables you to do the best kind of a job at a fair price. It creates goodwill while you give the customer a quality job.

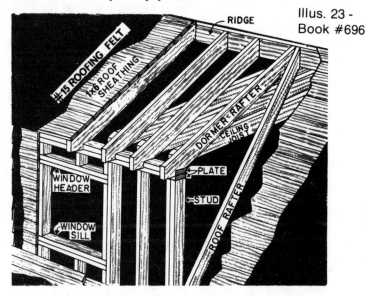

Illus. 23 - Book #696

If asphalt, asbestos, slate or tile roofing is to be applied, the roof is sheathed with solid sheathing. Most older houses were sheathed with 1 x 6, as shown. Buildings during the past thirty years were sheathed with plywood.

Roofers are frequently in short supply and too busy to handle a small job, so this creates opportunity for those who want to get into the roofing business. Book #696 Roofing Simplified explains what every roofer needs to know. All who can read and are willing to follow accurate and well planned step-by-step direction can learn all about roofing repairs and reroofing as easily as they can learn to sew or drive a car.

Those living in suburban areas soon discover the astronomical cost for certain improvements and repairs force many homeowners to neglect even those that are vitally important. Come a March wind, a heavy rain or twister, and the damage can be extensive. Finding a roofer, willing to make a repair at a cost the owner can afford, generates a lot of new business.

As Book #696 clearly explains, many people have a phobia when it comes to height, even to climbing a ladder. Most fear walking and working on a roof. They believe it's a no man's land insofar as their capabilities are concerned.*

The first chapter of Book #696 explains how to make a rope body harness and a roofer's safety line. It explains how to anchor the safety line so no one can actually fall off a ladder or a roof. When the body harness is positioned and adjusted to fit, and the safety line is anchored as directions specify, climbing a ladder, walking and working on a roof is safer than crossing many city streets.

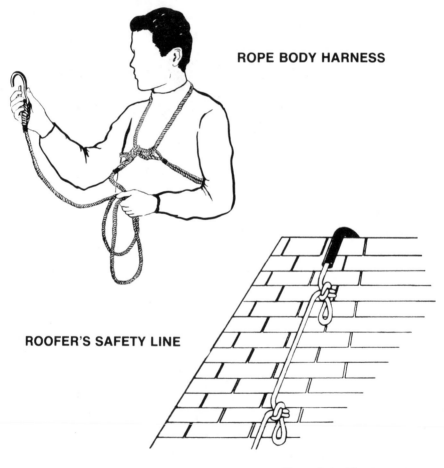

ROPE BODY HARNESS

ROOFER'S SAFETY LINE

Illus. 3,4 - Book #696

*Note warning on page 53.

Getting experience is essential. If you have no place to test your skill as a roofer, make the body harness and become thoroughly familiar with the roofer's safety line. When you phone an established roofer or retailer for an appointment, explain you are looking for work and would like to talk to whoever does the hiring. You will get the most favorable response shortly after a storm has done considerable damage. Homeowners and pros give more consideration when the need is urgent. In each interview, regardless of whether it's a homeowner, retailer or roofing contractor, speak up and state you know how to walk and work on a roof in complete safety, can make needed roofing and gutter repairs, and are willing and able to follow direction. Regardless of what they say, few roofers can find applicants with this capability. Most applicants chicken out when they have to climb an extension ladder, let alone walk and work on a roof. Tell each prospective employer you have a roofer's safety line and body harness. While few skilled roofers use these, they realize a new employee might prove an insurance liability without one.

Visit home improvement centers and note the various kinds of roofing sold. Get a copy of the manufacturer's application instructions. These provide much helpful information. While many will seem technical in nature, after reading Book #696 you will be able to intelligently talk to that retailer or roofing contractor. You must accentuate their confidence in you.

One way to obtain prospective customers is to contact each home improvement center that sells roofing. While many only sell material, others sell labor and material. If a local retailer feels he has all the roofing personnel he needs, and a roofer gives you a hard time saying, "We only hire skilled roofers or selected apprentices," offer your service in a letter to homeowners in good neighborhoods. Stuff every roadside mailbox with an 8½ x 11" handbill. Use the same message roofers insert in the yellow pages of a telephone directory.

```
┌─────────────────────────────────────────┐
│                                         │
│   WE MAKE ROOFING REPAIRS               │
│   PROTECT YOUR INVESTMENT               │
│                                         │
│            Re-roofing,                  │
│         Gutters, Leaders,               │
│        Waterproof Basements             │
│    AT A COST YOU CAN AFFORD             │
│                                         │
│         No job too small.               │
│                                         │
│       We guarantee satisfaction.        │
│                                         │
│        We are insured roofers.          │
│         References supplied.            │
│                                         │
│      Phone for a free estimate.         │
│                                         │
│                                         │
│               NAME                      │
│             ADDRESS                     │
│              PHONE                      │
│                                         │
└─────────────────────────────────────────┘
```

Prior to, or at the start of the rainy season, place a flyer in every mailbox in that part of town where a previous wind or rain has done the most damage. When a TV station or newspaper shows storm damage, note the neighborhoods covered. Nature generates much fear and seeds many customers. Harness this power, it can be your best salesman.

If you decide to go into the roofing business, it's essential to talk to an insurance agent. You need insurance that protects a customer against any damage that may occur while you are on their property. A knowledgeable owner will ask the name of the company, policy number and amount of coverage it provides before agreeing to your doing any work.

To ascertain what local competition may charge for a comparable job, get someone, preferably an elderly person living alone, to go through the yellow pages and invite bids for a "roofing job." The estimates explain how competition stays in business, even when they don't work too often. As Better Business Bureau case studies indicate, con artists still operate in the home repair and improvement arena.

Don't expect to make a sizeable profit on your first few jobs. Use these to gain experience. If you lack money for material, tell the customer what you need. Explain you are just starting and need the work. Many will be agreeable to buying everything the job requires. If you average only a minimum hourly wage rate, it could still prove a sound investment of time.

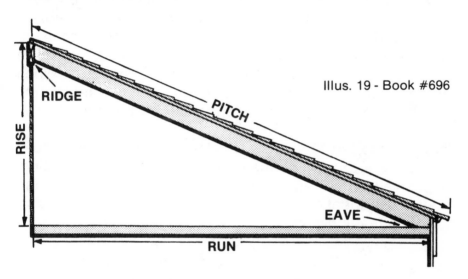

Illus. 19 - Book #696

The kind of roofing selected, and manner in which it's applied is dependent on the "pitch" of the roof. The "pitch" is the angle of rafter. The "rise" is the vertical distance between the eave and top of ridge. The "run" is the distance rafter covers from plate at eave to ridge.

To get a logical picture as to what your services are worth, and what to charge, spend the necessary time to get as many estimates as you can from those specializing in the same area of repair. Be sure to check discount and chain store prices. If you want to find out what a roofer will charge to apply a certain grade of asphalt shingle over existing shingles, tell him the overall length of roof, pitch and width, note Book #696 Roofing Simplified.

Solving Neighborhood Problems

All who own a home know problems keep surfacing constantly. Cracks in a concrete walk, a clogged drain or settling in a foundation can allow water into a basement. During a heavy rain, flooding frequently occurs. Become a specialist in the repair of foundations. Learning to seal cracks in a concrete floor, walk or foundation wall, analyzing what needs to be done and how to perform each step, provides unlimited opportunity. A flyer stuffed in all mailboxes, particularly after a heavy rain, will usually result in developing some interested prospects. Houses located in low areas invariably face "wet basement problems." When you do work for one customer, you often find others in the neighborhood waiting to have the same job done.

Two books, #617 Concrete Work Simplified and #697 Forms, Footings, Foundations, Framing, Stair Building, explain everything you need to know to seal, waterproof, and insulate foundation walls. This is an area of prime importance to many owners.

These two books will also prove of special interest to all who see potential in building additions, garages, etc.

While most problems stem from a clogged gutter, leader or drain tile to a dry well, others require waterproofing a foundation. Always start by cleaning a gutter, leader and drain pipe to dry well. When these are free of debris, use a garden hose to check gutters. Keep water running to make certain leaders handle runoff. If dampness appears in basement, recommend a foundation waterproofing job as explained in Books #617 and 697.

As more and more homeowners recognize the income potential in modernizing a basement, they realize it's essential to keep it dry.

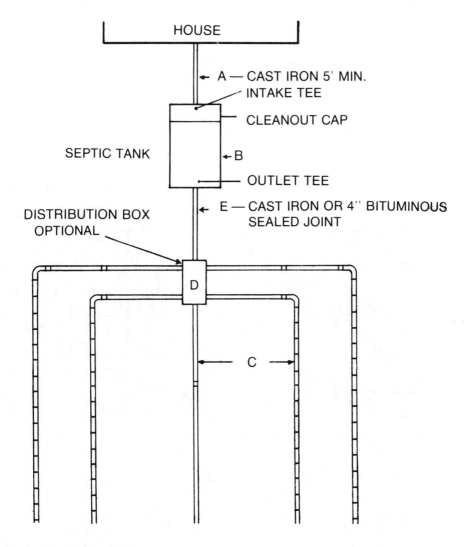

HOUSE

A — CAST IRON 5' MIN.
INTAKE TEE

CLEANOUT CAP

SEPTIC TANK

B

OUTLET TEE

E — CAST IRON OR 4'' BITUMINOUS
SEALED JOINT

DISTRIBUTION BOX
OPTIONAL

D

C

Illus. 184 - Book #617

Many homeowners, living in areas where waste is handled by a septic tank, find it necessary to put in a new tank and field when they build an addition. Complete details for installation of the tank and field is explained in Book #617.

As inflation destroys the purchasing power of the dollar, it emphasizes the sound value of real estate. It also conditions prospective customers to the many reasons the repairs you propose are essential.

Many top executives who face too much stress in their work discover concrete work and bricklaying a great way to relax. Winston Churchill was famous for his ability both as a leader and a bricklayer. He laid bricks everytime he had an opportunity to relax from his superhuman endeavors.

Illus. 65,161,132 - Book #668

Book #668 Bricklaying Simplified provides much helpful information. It explains how to mix mortar, the use of brick ties in building walls, brick facing a house, laying brick walks, patios, easy to build barbecues, brick tree wells and more.

Learning any trade, whether it's bricklaying, carpeting or concrete work, doesn't require any special skill. It does require reading how it's done, then making certain you know every step. As with each book, #683 Carpeting Simplified provides all the information anyone needs. It explains what tools are required, where same can be rented, how, when and where each should be used.

Using a stretcher as illustrated simplifies making a tight and straight installation.

Illus. 92 - Book #683

Retailers of products that require installation seldom have a sufficient number of skilled personnel. Since installation costs frequently discourage a sale, retailers continually seek skilled personnel willing to work at a cost the customer can afford. You never know which retailer, ceramic tile, carpeting, paneling, etc., needs help until you ask. To gain experience fast, make an installation in your home. If this isn't possible, take a job as an assistant. Working alongside a pro can prove extremely helpful.

It's Easy and Profitable

Job opportunities surface everytime anyone needs any work done and is either incapable or unwilling to do it. Many older people are physically unable to do what needs to be done. Living on fixed incomes, they find comfort in owning their home and greatly appreciate the importance of keeping it in repair. They value its warmth, security and protection. When window screens blacken, and gaping holes allow insects, wasps and flys to roam at will, replacement of screening is essential. Offering to "REPLACE WORN SCREENING," with a flyer stuffed in mailboxes, can earn an immediate profit in the screens you repair.

Place a flyer in all mailboxes, then visit with every home-owner who is working outside, telephone or try making house calls. The flyer frequently acts as a "door opener."

NEED NEW SCREENS?

We replace worn screening.
Frames repaired, refinished
or replaced when necessary

AT A COST YOU CAN AFFORD

We use top quality screening,
your choice of
aluminum, copper of fiberglass.

We guarantee satisfaction.

References supplied.
Phone for a free estimate.

NAME
ADDRESS
TELEPHONE

While fiberglass screening is very popular, many customers still prefer aluminum or copper. Always show customers samples of all three. Let them select.

To obtain the best possible price, you will have to buy screening to a width that allows for the least amount of waste, in fifty or sixty foot rolls. In estimating customer cost for material needed, i.e., screening, moldings, paint, angle braces, etc., you must also include waste due to size of frame and material needed for grippers plus a profit. When added to the time (labor) required to repaint and apply new screening and, where necessary, new moldings, you begin to total customer costs.

Prior to quoting an estimate for replacing the screening, ascertain what local or chain stores charge for a comparable size screen. Also check the yellow pages to see what home improvers mention doing this work. Few will quote any costs over the phone. Most want to see the condition of the frames. Even more important, they want to "case" the property and appraise how much or how little a customer knows about what needs to be done.

To make an honest estimate, it's necessary to actually replace some screens and keep an accurate check on the time each step requires. Add 25 to 40% to the cost of screening. This usually provides a safe margin to cover waste, grippers, etc. Add labor at whatever rate you believe is fair.

Number each frame and window as it's removed from a window. Always replace each frame in its original position. When necessary, indicate top of frame.

Remove existing screen molding carefully. Always pry molding alongside a brad. If paint and brads have welded the molding in place, try other end and work down. Save all good screen molding. Buy new screen molding where necessary. Two screwdrivers are usually all you need to pry up molding. Don't force molding.

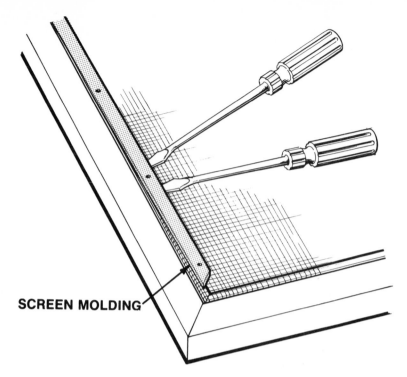

SCREEN MOLDING

Number molding as you remove same. For example, on screen No. 1, number the left verticle L1, the right vertical R1. This insures replacing molding in proper position and screen.

After removing screen moldings, old screening, staples or nails, check frame to make certain it's square. (Measure diagonals.) If necessary, apply corner plates or angles.

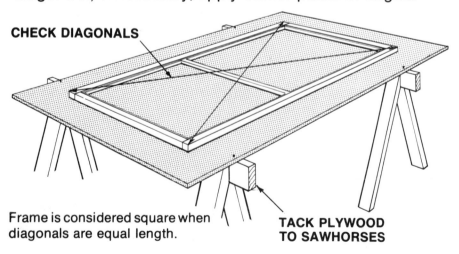

CHECK DIAGONALS

Frame is considered square when diagonals are equal length.

TACK PLYWOOD TO SAWHORSES

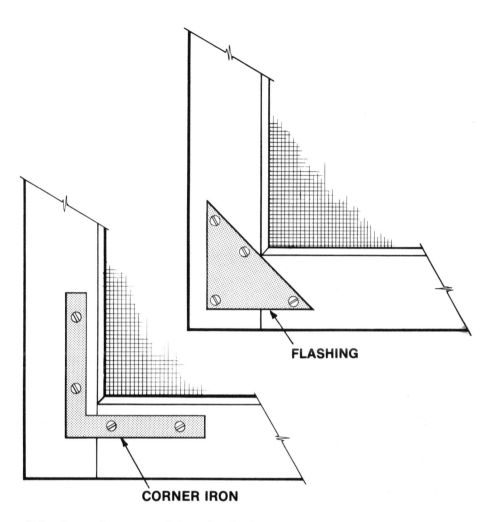

FLASHING

CORNER IRON

Windows in most older single family houses were protected with frames made from 5/4 x 2". At one time, 5/4" in these frames measured a full 1¼" thick. Today 5/4" measures approximately 1 1/16". In the majority of cases, these frames are reusable. Some may need the corners stiffened, new screen molding, etc. Applying an L-angle or a copper or aluminum flashing cut to shape shown will hold a frame square.

To replace screening like a pro, and do a top job in as little time as possible, it's necessary to set up a ½ or ⅝", 4 x 5 or 6' plywood panel on a workbench or on two sawhorses. Clamp or temporarily toenail the plywood in place.

133

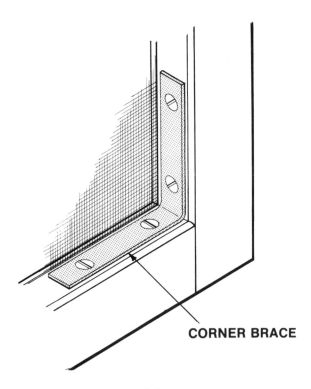

CORNER BRACE

If diagonals aren't equal, stand frame on one corner and tap diagonally opposite corner gently. When frame is square, screw the corner plates in position. When using a surface bracket, fasten in position shown so it doesn't prevent frame from fitting snugly in position. At this point paint frames.

Since most homes contain different size screens, a 4 x 5' or 4 x 6' plywood layout table permits screwing stops in position required. You can use 1 x 2 stops for a 5/4 x 1'' thick frame. Always use a stop of equal or less than thickness of frame. Don't allow screws or nails used to fasten stops project above as this frequently can damage a piece of screening.

Place 1 x 2 A and B stops in position. Check with square. The jig stops must be square. Always place frame in position and nail stops as shown. Check diagonals of stops to make certain they are square. Only place frame in a jig when it's square, then fasten stops C and D securely to hold in place.

134

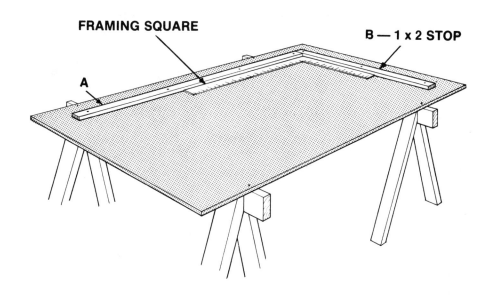

FRAMING SQUARE

B — 1 x 2 STOP

A

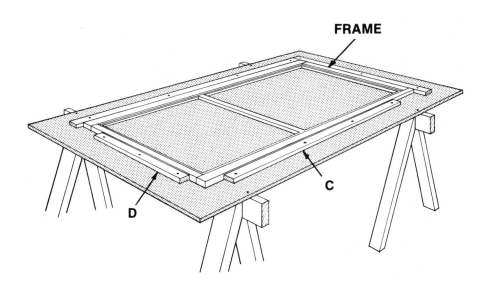

FRAME

C

D

135

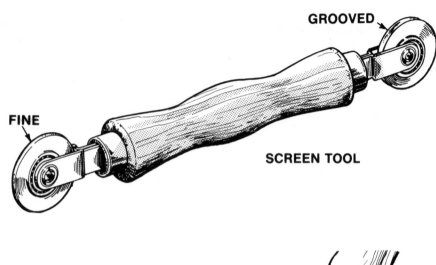

GROOVED

FINE

SCREEN TOOL

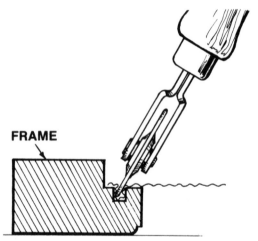

FRAME

Most wood and all aluminum screen frames contain a slot for the screening. Forcing the screening into this slot, while keeping the wire parallel to frame, is important. A screening tool simplifies this. The tool has both a fine and a grooved wheel. You use the fine wheel to force screening into slot, the grooved wheel to force the spline in an aluminum screen.

While most wood screens have slots, if the screen doesn't have a slot, staple left vertical side first. Nail molding in position.

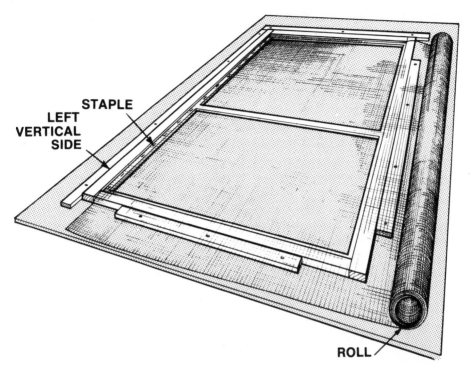

STAPLE

LEFT
VERTICAL
SIDE

ROLL

Using roll of wire, stretch screen taut. Use fine wheel to force right side in slot and staple screen in position. Apply molding to right side. Always make certain screening remains square to frame.

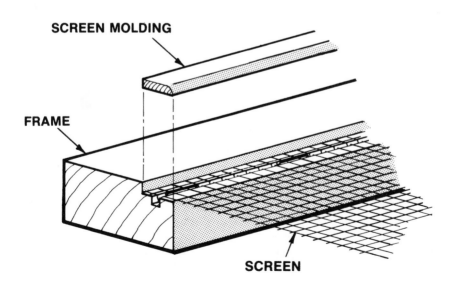

SCREEN MOLDING

FRAME

SCREEN

137

Keeping wire parallel to top, staple screen and apply molding. All overage projecting beyond molding can be cut later with a razor blade knife.

Apply pressure and pull screen taut. Staple bottom. Apply molding and cut overage.

As previously mentioned, always number each window and each screen. While most wood screens have hangers screwed to tops, it's frequently necessary to indicate TOP on aluminum screens as each is removed and numbered.

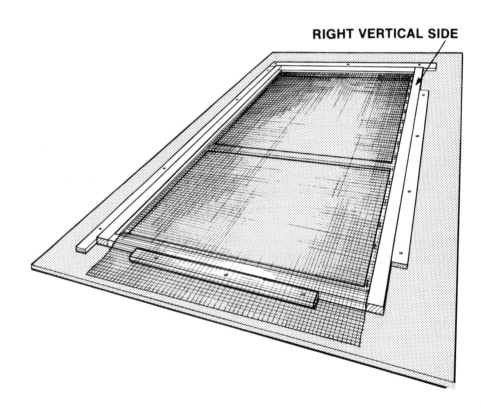

RIGHT VERTICAL SIDE

Aluminum Frame Screens

After removing metal or plastic splines, remove old screening. Wire brush slot. Steel wool frame. Medium grade will brighten an old aluminum frame. Always use aluminum screening, never copper, in an aluminum frame.

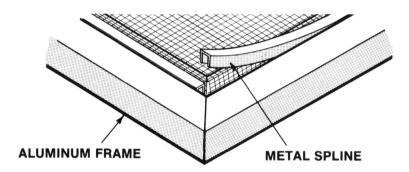

ALUMINUM FRAME   **METAL SPLINE**

Replacing screening in an aluminum frame requires ⅜" stops on both sides of frame. Use ⅜" strips of plywood or ⅜" lathe.

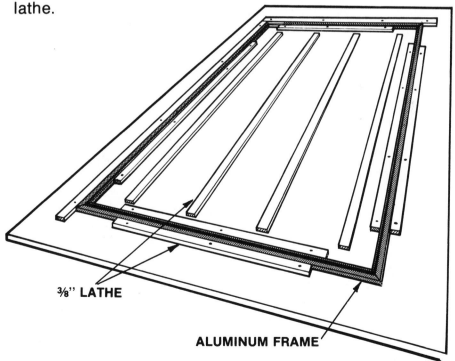

⅜" LATHE

ALUMINUM FRAME

To prevent the screening from laying loose in the middle of a large frame, place ⅜" thick lathe or plywood strips in position shown.

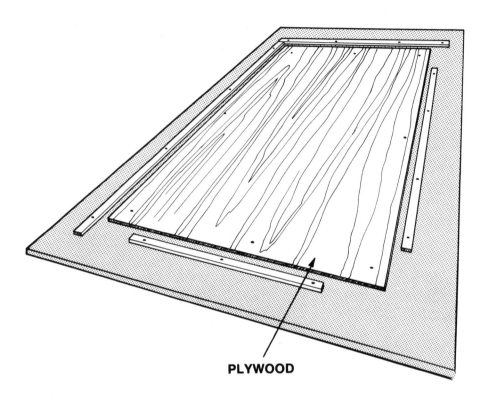

PLYWOOD

NOTE: Those contracting a school, factory, office or other large installation where many screens of one size need replacing, should cut a piece of plywood to full size inside dimension of frame opening. Use thickness of plywood that equals thickness of aluminum frame. Check diagonals of plywood to make certain it's square. Brad this plywood to work table.

Fasten equal thickness stops on outside. This not only keeps a frame square, but also holds it rigidly in position as you force screening into slot with the fine wheel on the wheel groover.

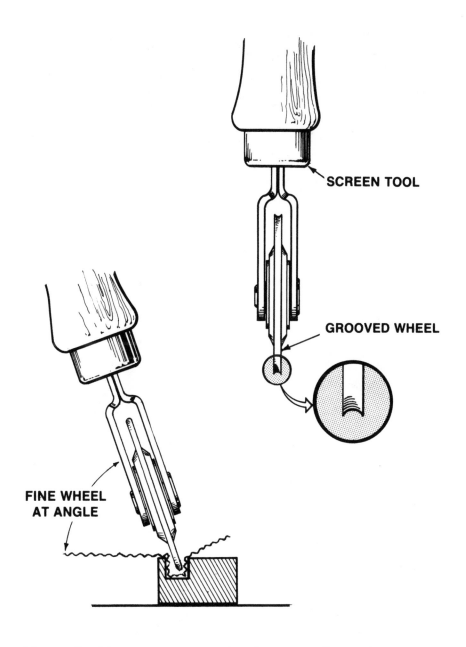

SCREEN TOOL

GROOVED WHEEL

FINE WHEEL AT ANGLE

Always hold groover at angle shown so fine wheel forces screening against bottom outside edge of slot.

Most pros cut screening off roll after right spline has been forced into place using grooved wheel. Be sure to keep screen wire parallel to frame.

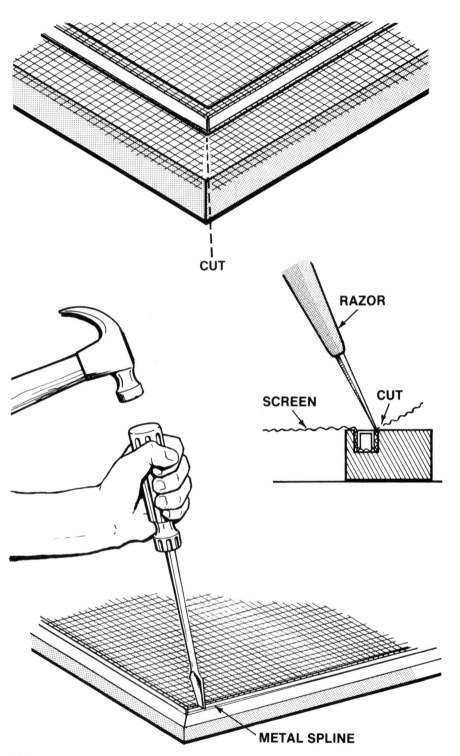

CUT

RAZOR

SCREEN   CUT

METAL SPLINE

Stretch wire over right slot. Use fine wheel to force screening in slot. Insert right spline using grooved wheel.

Prior to forcing ends of spline in place, make a diagonal cut in screening from outer edge of slot at corner. Use a screw driver and hammer to force end of spline in flush with frame.

NOTE: Many metal splines have mitered ends so it's necessary to replace each in proper position.

In many cases, old metal splines will bend and twist on removal. While these can be reused by carefully starting one end in proper position, then positioning and forcing spline back into slot, in some cases, you may first have to spread the spline slightly. This enables it to grip when forced in.

Always position holes in spline for window opener in exact position shaft of opener and screw holes require before forcing metal spline in position.

If a metal spline isn't reuseable, buy plastic or rubber spline to size slot requires. Take a piece of the metal spline along to make certain you buy proper size.

When aluminum screens are placed on the inside of a window and the window opener goes through the spline and frame, always save a sufficient length of metal spline so it can be used. A 6 to 8" length, drilled to receive screws holding opener in place greatly simplifies installation. Use plastic spline on balance of window.

Using a razor blade knife, cut overage from outside edge of spline.

Since many people need screening replaced, it offers an opportunity to make meaningful and profitable contacts. While doing the work, keep an eye open for termites and flying ants. You can generate an even bigger job termite-proofing the premises.

Termites and Ants
Create New Business

A man's home may be his castle, but that doesn't discourage invasion by unwanted and very destructive occupants. Come spring, termites and flying ants start to surface while the balance of the year they keep hidden, busily eating away sills, headers and joists. In some places they leave evidence, a trail of sawdust and droppings. In many others, working within concealed areas, they quietly destroy framing. Only when a floor starts to loosen or sag, or exterior or interior wall covering starts to loosen, does the homeowner realize what is happening. When an experienced buyer begins to appraise the value of a home and is permitted to poke a penknife into sills, headers or the outside ends of joists, does the full impact of the damage become apparent. Replacing destroyed framing can be costly.

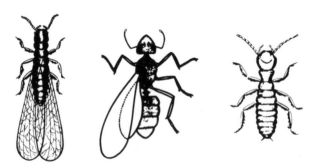

The easiest way to distinguish between a winged termite (left) and a winged ant (center) is by the termite's thicker waist. Winged termites spawn colonies of wingless workers (right).

Homeowners who call in a franchised termiteproofing company frequently get a shock. Recognizing how little the owner knows, they accentuate their fears to justify quoting an estimate for "termiteproofing the house." Many base total costs on what they think the traffic will bear. A "fast buck operator" doesn't plan on establishing a lasting relationship. Since a satisfied customer is one of your best assets, level with each customer. Explain what must be done. Tell them you can impregnate the soil around the entire perimeter of the house or currently affected areas.

Termiteproofing can prove a profitable service and still give each customer a fair deal. Every contact enables you to analyze other needs, replace screening, painting, chimney cleaning, etc. Always stress "preventative maintenance" when offering to termiteproof any area.

Franchised termiteproofers invariably base their estimate on saturating the entire perimeter, when, in many cases, only a limited area, one or two rooms, may indicate activity. Since few homeowners know how much scrap wood was buried during the filling and grading process, and no one can be certain exactly where termite and ant colonies are located, a perimeter saturation is always the safest and costliest. Saturating the area outside the affected rooms invariably eliminates the problem at much less than half the cost of a perimeter job.

Most customers report an ant or termite infestation in a kitchen. Saturating the foundation area outside the kitchen usually destroys these nests. If a flagstone terrace is outside, each stone should be raised and/or moved to permit proper saturation. Only move one flagstone at a time so after saturation it can be replaced in proper position. As each is raised you see more or fewer ants or termites. Since many homeowners are physically unable, or don't have the time to do what needs to be done, when you hear of an owner with an ant problem they haven't been able to eliminate with a powder or trap, recommend an ant and termiteproofing job.

Where you have to raise flagstones, you see more and more ants and termites as you get close to a nest. After saturating this area, keep lifting stones and saturating soil until you begin lifting flagstone that's completely free.

145

Most well stocked hardware and home centers sell the Ross Soil Injector Tool and chemical tablets recommended for ants and termites.

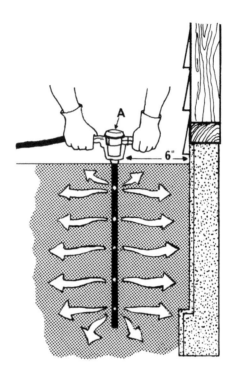

The tool contains a mixing chamber in the head. Place three tablets in the chamber. Connect the tool to a garden hose. Holes in bottom of tube allow treated water to saturate the soil. Drive the tube into the soil within 6" of the foundation. Turn water on and slowly raise the rod. Use three tablets to saturate each lineal foot around affected area.

When you reach the surface, open valve slowly to saturate surface. Only open valve a wee bit so as not to spray the mixture on your shoes and clothing.

NOTE: Always wear gloves. Don't allow any of the mixture to come in contact with your skin or clothes. If any gets on your skin, wash immediately using soap and water.

If the area next to the house is covered with a concrete walk, it's usually necessary to drill holes 6'' from foundation, one foot apart. Insert injector and saturate subsoil. You will have to rent an electric hammer to drill holes. Inspect the job a week later to make certain no ants or termites are still alive, then mix one part cement to two parts of sand and close up holes in concrete.

Illus. 45 - Book #617

If the tube can be inserted between a concrete or flagstone walk and foundation, this frequently enables you to saturate a colony.

While franchised operators invariably promote "perimeter saturation" and can justify recommending same, we think it's better to explain the facts to each customer. In this way you can solve more problems for more people at less cost to each, make a profit on each job and still feel sure the customer will call you back if the ants or termites surface in another area.

Easy to Sell Enclosure

Everyone of every age can find a profitable use of time if they do two things: Find and fill a need. A case in point is the garbage can enclosure. This doesn't require a lot of capital or a workshop containing special tools. If you have access to a saw, hammer and drill, building and delivering these containers to the buyer can produce a steady volume of profitable business.

The container shown was designed to accommodate two cans. A stretched out version can be built by adding multiples of 24" to the front, back and lid for each can. Active block associations in some cities now sponsor the use of these containers curbside to accommodate plastic garbage bags. These must be placed with lid opening on roadside to facilitate emptying.

Since every family likes to eat, and garbage is a necessary part of the living process, protecting cans against marauding dogs, cats, even racoons, while eliminating an eyesore, has natural appeal.

For a two can container, you will need the following:
1 — ⅝" x 4 x 8' plywood
1 — ⅝" x 2 x 4' plywood (good one side)
1 — 1 x 4 x 6'
1 — 2 x 4 x 8'
3 — 1 x 2 x 10'
3 — 3" T-hinges with 6 — ¾" No. 7 screws
1 — 2" hasp with 7 — ⅝" No. 4 screws
4 — ⅜" Teenuts
4 — ⅜ x 1" machine bolts

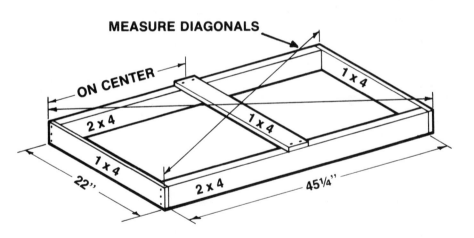

Cut 1 x 4 and 2 x 4 to size indicated. Nail 1 x 4 to 2 x 4 with three 6 penny nails. Check corners with a square or measure diagonals. Frame is square when diagonals are equal in length. Before nailing 1 x 4 across top center, drill four ½" holes, ½" deep in position shown.

149

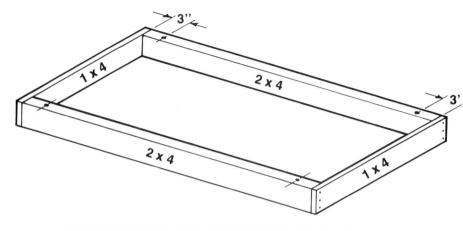

LOCATE ½" HOLE FOR TEENUT IN BOTTOM OF 2 x 4

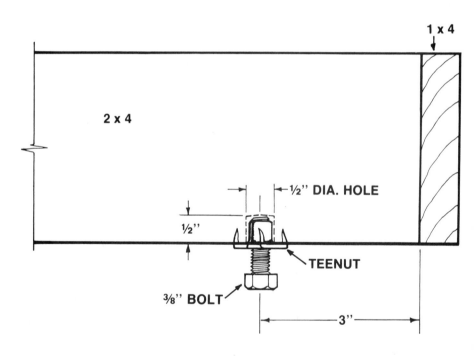

Drive Teenuts into each hole. Turn frame over and nail 1 x 4 at center.

150

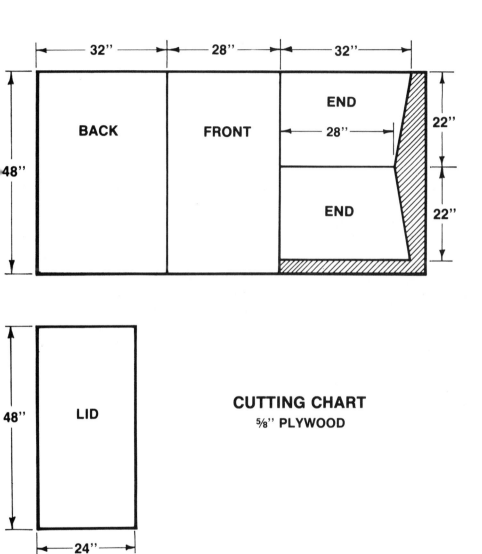

CUTTING CHART
⅝" PLYWOOD

Cut ⅝" plywood for front, back and ends to size and shape shown from 4 x 8 panel. Cut lid from 2 x 4 panel.

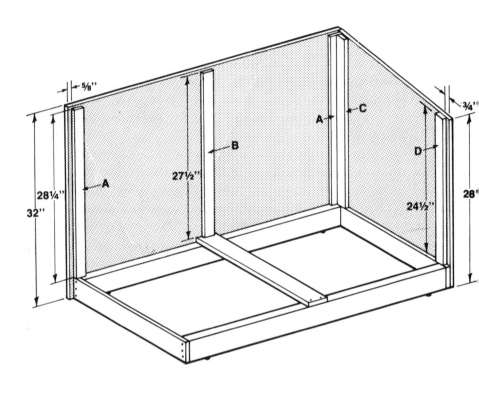

Cut two A - 1 x 2 x 28¼'', one B - 1 x 2 x 27½'', two C - 1 x 2 x 28¼'', two D - 1 x 2 x 24½'', two E - 1 x 2 x 24½'', one F - 1 x 2 x 23¾'', three G - 1 x 2 x 18''. Nail A,B,C,D,E,F in position shown using 3 penny common nails.

For a three can container, cut front and back 72''; for a four can container, cut front and back 96''. Nail B, F and G in position shown. Add extra hinges.

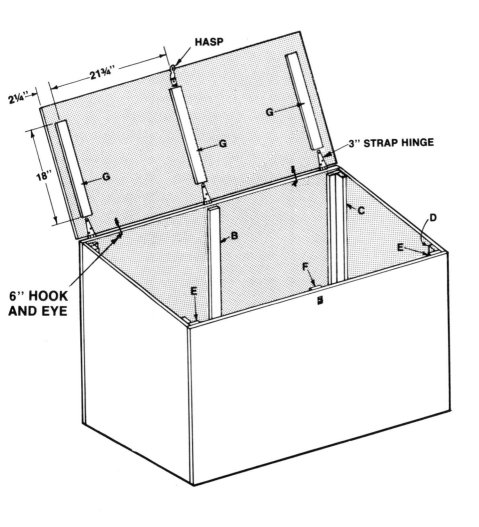

Nail ends to base frame. Nail back to base and to C using 6 penny nails. Nail front to base and to D.

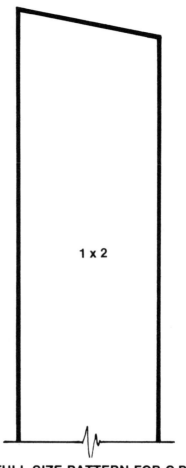

FULL SIZE PATTERN FOR C,D

Cut C and D to angle of ends.

Nail 1 x 2 G to lid in position shown with 3 penny nails. Fasten three 3" light strap hinges to back and inside of lid in position shown. Fasten hooks and eyes in position shown to keep lid open.

Fasten hasp to lid and hook to front.

While many garden supply, hardware and home centers will act as sales agents, most will want a display sample on consignment. This means you only bill them when it's sold. It remains your property. Since few will want to stock containers, you will find it necessary to deliver same to the

154

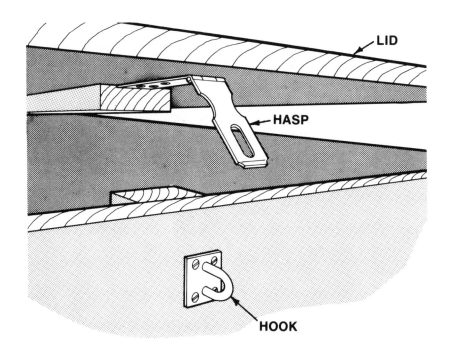

customer. Depending on size these boxes sell for $69.00 to $100.00. They offer a good return on time invested.

The retailer will want anywhere from 15 to 25% of the retail price for making the sale. Since you must invest money in material and make a profit on material, plus labor, and assume cost of delivering, your best bet is to sell direct to customers by offering same in flyers stuffed in all mailboxes.

Prior to making delivery, ask the customer if they want the box painted to match their house. While this adds to its cost, many prefer having it done.

Place the box where customer requests, then level box by inserting 1" machine bolts in Teenuts.

Always ask each customer whether they know anyone who might also be interested. And, as previously mentioned, note the condition of their screens, inquire whether they have had any problem with ants or termites, etc.

Build and Sell Greenhouses

Wherever you see a house you can find at least one plant lover. Building two different priced window greenhouses and two walk-in models can earn a lot of green. Since plant lovers live everywhere, the sales potential is unlimited. Step-by-step directions contained in Book #811 explain how to build low cost window greenhouses as well as the most expensive models, a walk-in greenhouse, sunhouse, plus electric light gardening. There's something for everyone regardless of whether they live in an apartment or a house. This book simplifies building and installing greenhouses to any size window. These provide considerable growing space plus a solar heating capability. When fastened to a first floor window, it adds a sizeable measure of protection.

A wood sided, plastic covered greenhouse costs little to build. It can be sold at a good profit.

The aluminum framed, glass or acrylic greenhouse allows you to sell for ½ to ⅔ less than those offered by out of town manufacturers.

Illus. 3,4 - Book #811

Illus. 9 - Book #811

A walk-in greenhouse can be constructed alongside a basement door or window. Those who wish to grow tall plants can build to overall height they prefer. Where no basement window or door is available, building alongside a first floor window provides sufficient heat to keep the proper temperature all winter.

Book #811

Those who recognize the savings in harnessing solar heat find the 7 x 7'0'' or 7 x 14'0'' walk-in greenhouse or sunhouse an ideal collector. When sheathed with the proper plastic, glass or acrylic, it attracts those who enjoy sunbathing all winter. Motels with indoor pools find sunhouses have great rental appeal to winter guests. While few sunhouses permit getting a Florida tan, being able to lay out in the sun on a cold, clear, winter day has great appeal.

Illus. 169 - Book. #811

A sizeable market also exists for the easy to build toolhouse described in Book #811. As more and more people retire, finding a constructive use of time manufactures many customers. While the book simplifies building a 6'0" x 7'9" toolhouse, directions also explain how to lengthen it to size desired. This structure provides instant relief for all the gardening tools that usually clutter up a garage. It also makes an ideal hobby shop, one that accommodates a workbench or photo darkroom.

Illus. 171 - Book #811

Parents interested in keeping children playing in their own backyard find a playhouse has great appeal. Many will buy a toolhouse plus an extra set of playhouse doors. Children like the play-store door. Since it's vitally important to supervise a child's activities, the low door and large window eliminate any secluded areas. Stress this point when discussing the sale of a playhouse-toolhouse with each customer. Offer the playhouse door as an accessory. When the child outgrows the playhouse, the counter doors are removed and the hinges are used to hang the toolhouse doors.

Always keep in mind each customer contact has great potential. You never really know all their conscious and sub-conscious needs. Those who go into the greenhouse, sunhouse, toolhouse business soon discover they can sell the same customers curved back, curved seat lawn chairs, settees and four passenger lawn gliders as described in Book #754. As the cost of gasoline discourages the use of a car, people spend more time at home. Furniture that encourages outdoor living has special appeal.

To simplify construction of each piece, the book contains a large foldout pattern that provides full size outlines for each curved part.

Book #754

Create a Place to Work

Foldaway workbench only requires 6'' of floor space when not in use.

Illus. 19 - Book #672

The need to show a sample of everything you want to sell is all important. If you currently don't have a place to build, build a scale model. These not only build self confidence, but also make excellent sales tools.

One retiree wrote to tell how he had started a new business. Prior to retirement he had placed a scale model of the lawn chair, adult and child size workbench on his desk. As traffic manager of a large corporation, he was constantly discussing business with associates. Almost everyone picked up and examined the models. When informed he planned on

162

building these on retirement, he began getting orders. The night of his retirement party, he received fourteen orders for workbenches, plus seven orders for lawn chairs.

6' vise on both sides of top permits two to use workbench.

Illus. 165 - Book #672

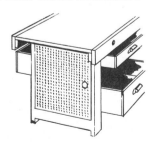

STORES HAND TOOLS IN END COMPARTMENT

VISE HOLDS LARGE PANELS

DRAWERS OPEN FROM BOTH SIDES

Seasonal Needs Stimulate Sales

Just as roofing repairs and roofing replacement jobs are plentiful after a high wind, heavy rain or a bad twister, so will a seasonal need materially affect any business you enter. An early spring and summer display of outdoor furniture, an early fall display of workbenches benefits materially from seasonal buying habits. Those who live alongside a well traveled road find these displays stop a lot of traffic.

Another element vitally important to the success of a new business can be found in getting an established retailer to cooperate in selling what you build. Get one and you invariably get others. Many garden supply centers cooperate in displaying walk-in and window greenhouses, toolhouses, outdoor furniture and workbenches. Be prepared to sell them display samples at a special price.

Motels with outdoor swimming pools frequently cooperate and will display lawn furniture. While it gets a lot of use, it also helps manufacture customers. Be sure a nameplate is attached to each piece, one that tells where it can be purchased.

Learning to live the kind of life that continually builds one's ego, self confidence, pride and bank account doesn't take luck. It requires doing something each day you didn't think you could do the day before. Research probing physical and mental health now confirms one's age can no longer be judged in years, but in interest. Tests have proved conclusively many in their twenties, thirties, forties and fifties were older, physically and mentally, than some in their sixties and seventies. Having an interest, a willingness to meet and solve problems, keeps the mind alert and the body far healthier than those who feel life has dealt them a dirty deal. Being willing and able to follow good direction is much like having a second brain. It can help create an image you will be proud to see in the mirror each morning. Best of all, results can be achieved in a relatively short span of time.

Never allow a fixation on a specified career dictate your adult life. An unsuccessful artist sometimes discovers he can eat and live a lot better when he starts laying brick. A bricklayer may discover he has great potential as a chef, singer or salesman. What at first may appear to be a bad piece of luck might just be the hand of fate trying to get you started on the best part of your life. If you happened to be a top rated student or star athlete during high school or college and haven't achieved similar status in your chosen profession, you naturally feel discouraged and tend to see a negative image where before you enjoyed the magic of positive acclaim. Starting a business with only an investment of time, and money for a limited amount of material needed to build, can open doors to an entirely new way of life.

Most little girls love dollhouses. Some remember these all through their lives. Book #753 How to Build Dollhouses and Furniture explains how to build three different dollhouses, plus fourteen pieces of dollhouse furniture.

Illus. 1 - Book #753

THE DREAM DOLLHOUSE

PACKAWAY DOLLHOUSE

**OPEN BACK
COLONIAL DOLLHOUSE**

Illus. 7,8,9 - Book #753

Valance Board

Colonial Step Stool

Colonial Cradle

Colonial Fireside Bench

Dining and Occasional Chairs

Drop Leaf Table

Corner Shelf

Cobblers Bench

Colonial Planter

China Cabinet   Corner Cupboard   Shaker Hutch   Montpelier Bookcase

MINIATURE DOLLHOUSE FURNITURE

Illus. 11 - Book #753

167

One reading proves this book contains no technical direction, no need for special tools, and that the time invested will produce expected results. Since dollhouses can be built in a one room apartment, a basement or garage, the amount of space or time of day or night is of little consequence. What's important is the result the effort produces. Those who don't build dollhouses find building the fourteen pieces of miniature furniture offers an antidote to stress, sleepless nights plus a profit.

Getting into the dollhouse business attracts companionship and is a cure for loneliness. Building dollhouses can also improve family relationships. If a family joins in its construction, it provides hours of complete escape from tension, while it gives each participant an opportunity to assess their capabilities. Encourage everyone to get into the act. Depending on age and dexterity, one can make frames, shingles, clapboard siding, curtains, drapes, carpeting or the miniature furniture from the full size patterns. This could seed a lifetime interest and a profitable business. One reader commented:

> "I can't remember when I've had more fun building and furnishing a dollhouse for our granddaughter. You are so right, it's the best therapy for getting a family together I have ever experienced. Only one problem. The dollhouse is so beautiful, my wife wants to keep it and neighbors want to buy it. Guess we will have to continue building."

Building and selling dollhouses can be started in several different ways. Those in the city find many apartment dwellers prefer buying a kit of all parts cut to exact size required. Since this requires no costly packing and shipping charges, or the use of power tools, it offers a sizeable potential market. Since dollhouses have mass appeal, the three offered attract considerable interest and orders.

Collectors and Retailers
Share a Common Need

Those who build dollhouses and dollhouse furniture soon discover a profitable market exists for the museum quality acrylic display cases that can be built by following directions in Book #792 How to Build Collectors' Display Cases. Collectors of china, silver, emblems, antique dolls, tin toys, etc., etc., are a special breed who have learned to refocus their mind's eye on an area of interest that provides peace of mind. Displaying what they collect adds pleasure and pride to their effort. As directions simplify building all types of cases, the potential is unlimited. Every retailer buys display cases to display, store and sell perfumes, handbags, jewelry, etc. Offer to build to any size the retailer needs. And remember, he pays no costly packing and shipping charges.

Book #792

Directions simplify building a see through, sliding door display case, measuring 14½ x 44 x 75½'' or to size required.

The nation is currently investing big money purchasing collectibles of every kind. Many view these investments as inflationproof. Results from recent auction sales indicate they guessed right.

The display cases offered in Book #792 appeal to every collector as readily as they do gift, jewelry, antique and department stores. Each frames the article in the same way a picture is framed. Step-by-step directions show everyone interested how to turn acrylic into a fun way to earn income. As packing and shipping costs on these cabinets are excessively high, when acrylic is purchased locally, fabricated into a cabinet to exact size customer requests, then delivered, with no need for a costly carton and padding, your price can be much less than competition and still insure a sizeable margin of profit.

To make a meaningful, time saving presentation of your craftsmanship, note the merchandise a retailer features in advertising. Show the store display manager a photo, a scale model or a finished sample of an acrylic fixture that complements the product. If he likes what he sees, the manager will invariably recommend changes in overall size or shape. Encouraging a prospective client (the display manager) to suggest changes builds the ego, generates those positive vibrations essential to the success of every business transaction. Every retailer can either use the cases for merchandise display or sell to customers who collect.

Create a Spark and Fire an Interest

One's health, happiness and destiny are controlled entirely by one factor, i.e., how you use time. A teenager seeking work, a retiree climbing the walls with boredom, an executive under great stress, must discover a constructive use of time. Finding this provides Instant Escape without hitting a bottle.

Consider how one parent found release from tension while he helped shape the life of a son. The youth was shy, sensitive and about average in intelligence. He had difficulty mixing with children of his own age. When he read a newspaper story of a high flying kite, he became interested. He sent for the pattern and made the kite. It proved to be everything the article had said.

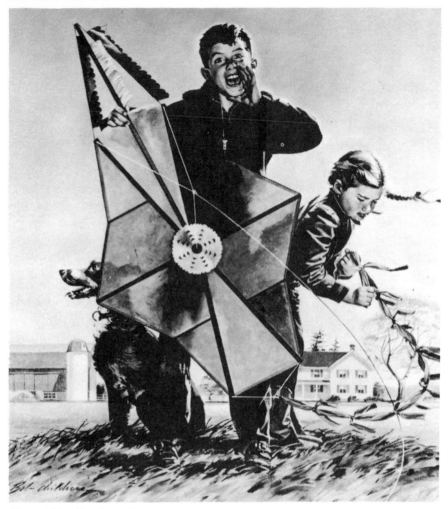

Illus. 151 - Book #771

The pattern for making this kite was easy to follow. On completion he became fascinated with its performance. He added extra "noise makers" and began to build additional ones with variations he found improved performance. The kites created so much interest he decided to manufacture for resale. These he sold to toy stores. Home centers began buying quantities to use as a sales promotional traffic builder.

172

Another letter told how a new business venture started in a similar manner.

"Living not too far from the Susquehanna, my son inherited his father's love for the water. Seeing your book on building kayaks in our local library, I borrowed it and was agreeably surprised to discover it triggered instant interest in my 15 year old."

The letter requested an order form and a few days later we received a check and order for the kayak book and several others. Almost a year later, we received a second letter that described how her husband and son had built the kayak, what fun and companionship it provided and how much more fun the youth had in using it.

"Since few kayaks are available in this area, it attracted so much attention my son is now spending all his free time building kayaks. He has begun to develop into quite a businessman. When anyone says they want to buy, he only starts building when a deposit sufficient to cover the cost of all material is advanced. In one case, the person didn't proceed with its purchase. Rather than be disappointed, he had no trouble selling it and making an even larger profit."

Illus. 1 - Book #757   Page 188 lists other easy to build boats.

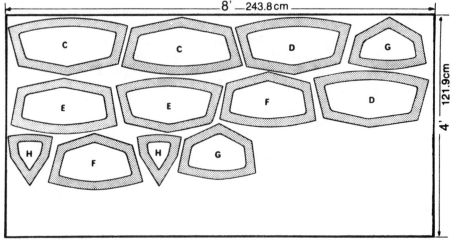

Frames for 16'9"

Illus. 11 - Book #757

Book #757 How to Build a Kayak not only contains easy to follow step-by-step directions, but also full size patterns that simplify tracing and cutting each different size frame, nose block, etc.

Encouraging someone to do something they have never previously attempted, providing a quality of direction that insures success, makes a magnetic and motivating contact. It's one that can shape the lifestyle of that individual. When this young man learned to build, use, sell and rent kayaks, he not only gained maturity, but also a sense of direction.

The kayak has special appeal to everyone of every age. Directions explain how to build three different lengths, 14'3", 16'9", 18'0". Extremely maneuverable and drawing little water, it can be used on lakes, inland waterways and, when properly handled, on many free flowing rivers.

Like jogging, kayaking is fast becoming a popular national pastime. Kayaks offer a quality of exhilerating exercise found in no other sport. Because of their light weight, even the 18' kayak can easily be transported on a car top luggage rack.

174

Learning to Earn in School

Concerned parents, who feel their youngster "has had it" with school, should talk to the vocational instructor. If their home needs a repair or improvement, obtain necessary direction, then ask the instructor to encourage your child to do what needs to be done. Consult the instructor for tools he may need. Repairs and improvements you need are frequently needed by other homes of the same vintage.

LEARN TO EARN courses are urgently needed. Encouraging a student to get on site job experience in their own home should be rated like other courses. Helping students solve a costly repair or improvement problem focuses their mind on a sphere of activity they can handle and take pride in doing. Learning to cook, sew, drive a car or perform any skill is part of the growing process. Turning that skill into work they enjoy, and earn money doing, should rate an A.

Homeowners, retailers, offices and factories, within a school district, should be contacted about part and full time jobs. All jobs should be posted on bulletin boards. Each school should mimeograph and post help wanted jobs so students seeking part time work know where to go and who to speak to. When a carpentry student likes carpentry, he should be encouraged to take part time jobs making carpentry repairs as a class project. With intelligent guidance, each could soon see a cash return for those after school hours invested.

A case in point is the outdoor display cabinet. These are popular with gift shop owners, realtors, gas station operators, as well as by homeowners who make and sell craft products. As reader mail confirms, when one is erected and put to use, others quickly see its potential. A recent letter described a basic sales concept few fully appreciate. When a gift or florist shop, ceramics, shoe or other type of retailer buys an outdoor display cabinet, take a picture to show retailers in neighboring towns.

Retailers, realtors and others who want to display photos or models of houses for rent or sale, can use either a bulletin board or an outdoor display cabinet. The bulletin board permits display of photos, the display cabinet scale models and goods.

Illus. 148,149 - Book #607

Regardless of what you offer, outdoor furniture, work-benches, bulletin boards, outdoor display cabinets, etc., note the yellow pages in the telephone book. It lists companies who specialize in printing limited quantities of either plastic or metal identification plates. These can mention your name, address and telephone number. Fasten one in an inconspicuous place to each piece and it soon seeds sales to other prospective customers.

Encouraging a youngster to "start a business," at the earliest possible age, provides survival insurance. Whether they run errands, take on a newspaper route, cut lawns, shovel snow, or wash cars, assuming responsibility helps build self confidence. It also acts as a conditioner, one that injects a habit called work into the body and brain of the individual. Each venture, whether it succeeds or fails, pays a dividend called experience. It also helps the individual recognize and appreciate how work dictates how they will live. Always encourage them. Every kind of work necessitates making contact with people.

Every consumer need creates a business opportunity for those who satisfy it. This basic fact of supply and demand is often overlooked by those who have the greatest need. Unemployed and facing mounting debt, many minds and marriages break. The individual sinks deeper and deeper into despair. It's at this point those capable of helping must make every effort to encourage a constructive use of time. Helping people find an interest, an activity that requires physical and mental effort, provides beneficial relief. Since everyone, of every age, will one day be subjected to these pressures, it's never too early to condition a mind. And the best way to make a constructive and motivating contact is by accentuating the positive.

Most children and those "young at heart" love a pet. Book #751 explains how to build a wide variety of pet housing. These shelters range from a doghouse, private and commercial type of kennel to a cat entry door through a basement window. This allows cat lovers to get a peaceful night's sleep. Directions also explain how to build a three room "catpartment," a special housing that permits your child to board a neighbor's cat without handling it. Directions also simplify building a parakeet cage, rabbit hutch and duck inn. Besides being able to sell this pet housing, directions explain how to board cats in the catpartment, dogs in the kennel, raise and sell rabbits, thereby cut food costs materially.

Encouraging even the youngest child to watch while you build a shelter for a pet, and, when old enough, to help, even if only to sandpaper a piece of wood, can shape a lifetime interest in carpentry. Every action you take to turn a child into an individual with interest and direction provides survival insurance.

DOG HOUSE

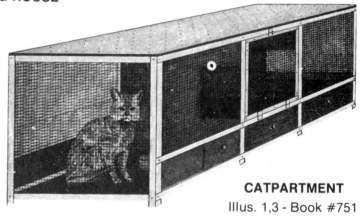

CATPARTMENT
Illus. 1,3 - Book #751

The three room catpartment is easy to build. The owner places the cat in the living-sleeping area. Adjoining rooms, one for feeding, the other for droppings, are accessible to the caretaker without having to handle the cat. Since cat lovers like to travel, the book suggests making contact with travel agents. Few real cat lovers will take a trip until they have found satisfactory shelter for their "loved ones."

Creating a cat boarding house by stacking catpartments, one over one, in a garage, can be started with one unit and one customer. It can be expanded as demand warrants same.

178

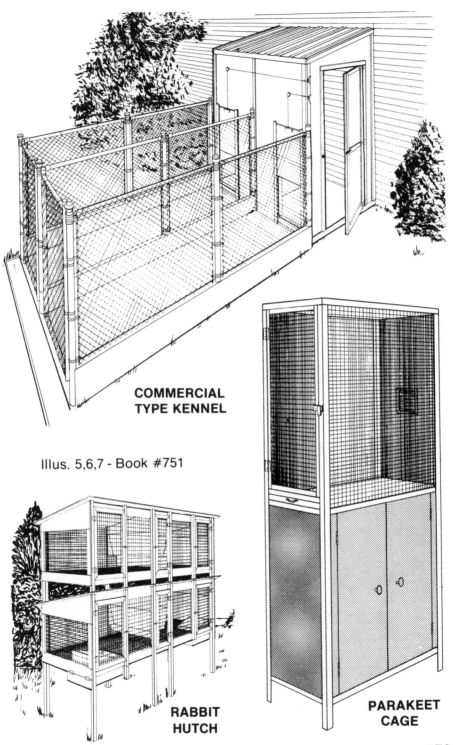

**COMMERCIAL
TYPE KENNEL**

Illus. 5,6,7 - Book #751

**RABBIT
HUTCH**

**PARAKEET
CAGE**

179

Canvas pet stores. Find out what type of pet they specialize in, then show a sample of the shelter designed for that pet. An intelligent pet store owner appreciates having a local source of supply since shipping costs on a comparable item could almost double its selling price.

Independently owned supermarkets interested in promoting the sale of pet foods, and well established pet stores will frequently display a pet housing unit to focus attention on selected products. Hardware stores find a parking lot display of the catpartment, parakeet cage, kennel, rabbit hutch, etc., a great way to stimulate the year round sale of wire fencing.

As food prices continue to climb, the eating habits of millions must be geared to what they can afford. More and more people are cultivating larger gardens. Thousands are discovering rabbits are easy to raise and can be bartered for

ALL WEATHER HOG HOUSE
Pattern #13

180

WESTCHESTER POULTRY HOUSE
Pattern #14

other meats. As Book #751 clearly explains, a doe will produce an average of five litters a year. When full grown, these are sold live to a local butcher who agrees to pay cash or credit against other meat. In 1977 over forty-five million pounds of rabbit meat was consumed, and the rate has been higher in recent years. Raising rabbit for the market helps shape a child's understanding of what living is all about.

Many homeowners, living in areas where zoning permits, are raising poultry and hogs. Building and selling these provide a lucrative market. The pattern method of construction lists what to buy, where and when each piece is used.

For The Parent Who Cares

Creating a bridge between a child's youth and the time he becomes a teenager offers once in a lifetime opportunity. Unless you help "grow them up" and assume responsibility, you suffer years of anguish. Encouraging a child to build birdhouses and birdfeeders, as explained in Book #669, can provide a richly rewarding experience. Learning to buy or scrounge for material that can be converted into a saleable birdfeeder or 16 room martin house offers an adventure in living. The child learns to meet people, to provide a service, to understand what the constructive use of time means.

Book #669

183

Christmas Generates Big Business

People love the spirit of Christmas and outdoor decorations have special appeal. Building and painting each decoration is greatly simplified by the full size patterns. These permit tracing the design, then painting it exactly as pattern indicates.

SANTA CLAUS Pattern #431

SANTA CLAUS SLEIGH
Pattern #434

CHRISTMAS REINDEER
Pattern #433

For an attractive display, combine Santa Claus, Reindeer and Sleigh.

LIFE SIZE NATIVITY SCENE Pattern #410
Camels available to add to display, Pattern #410C.

CHOIR BOYS GREETING
Pattern #562

JOLLY SNOWMEN
Pattern #331

TRY and you find The Real You

All who are out of work or dissatisfied with their present job, the size of their paycheck or prospects for the future, should recognize one fact of life. Worry over conscious and subconscious problems creates a massive source of energy. This power can produce an ulcer, nervous breakdown and suicide. It drives many to drink, drugs or crime. Only you can harness this power and put worry to work. Constantly complaining about a problem only time can help you resolve is like laying a sheet of metal across the negative and positive contacts in a 110 or 220 volt system. You get the shock of your life and blow a fuse. Accept whatever piece of hard luck you presently experience as par for the course called living. Refocus your mind on an entirely new sphere of activity. Everytime you feel yourself slipping, focus on the activity. Regardless of time, day or night, physically do something. As you begin to see progress, you automatically find yourself thinking more about it and not the problem. Learning to live is an interesting and exciting adventure.

Use this book as a surveyor uses a cornerstone. With direction you can accurately lay out a new life and achieve any goal you desire to reach. You can start at A and go into the attic modernization business and provide many elderly homeowners with space that can increase their monthly income. You can go to B and turn a basement into an income producing apartment or install extra bathrooms. Carpet retailers invariably find work for those who know how to lay carpeting. Whether you build dormers, make electrical repairs, install faucet washers, build garages or houses, directions are available to follow.

Converting time into a service or product, a creative and constructive activity, is something only YOU can do.

The following pages provide a quick reference guide to where you can find the needed direction to solve hundreds of problems — and make a profit on each job.

INDEX TO MONEY-SAVING REPAIRS, IMPROVEMENTS, PATTERNS AND BOOKS
(Number designates Easi-Bild Pattern or Book)

187

192

EASI-BILD® LEARN TO EARN BOOKS

#605 HOW TO INSTALL PANELING
Learn to apply paneling like a pro. Build a matching wall to wall storage closet with sliding doors, a fireplace mantel, install valances with indirect lighting, even build a cedar lined storage room. 146pp., 214 illus., plus full size valance patterns simplify every step.

#606 HOW TO LAY CERAMIC TILE
Easy to follow, step-by-step directions explain how to prepare a floor or wall prior to laying ceramic tile, how to estimate material needed, cut and fit tile around tub, toilet, etc. Read, learn, then see how easily you can make ceramic tile repairs like a pro. 98pp., 137 illus.

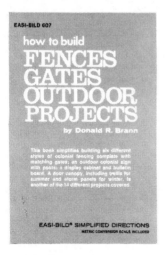

#607 HOW TO BUILD FENCES, GATES OUTDOOR PROJECTS
Every homeowner needs one or more of the improvements offered in this book. Every church, retailer, business, factory is a likely prospect for the outdoor display cabinet, bulletin board. 162pp., 212 illus.

#609 HOW TO BUILD AN ADDITION
Creating additional living space can prove to be one of today's soundest investments. Step-by-step directions explain how to build a 12 x 16', 16 x 24' or any other size one or two story addition, with or without an outside entry. 162pp., 211 illus., simplify every step.

#615 HOW TO MODERNIZE A BASEMENT

Whether you create a family room or turn a basement into an income producing one bedroom apartment with an outside entrance, you will find all the information needed. It explains how to install an outside entry, build stairs, frame partitions, panel walls, lay floor tile and much more. 98pp., 135 illus.

#617 CONCRETE WORK SIMPLIFIED

This book explains everything you need to know to mix concrete, floating, finishing, grooving, edging and pointing, to setting ironwork and anchor bolts. It also explains how to waterproof a basement, install a sump pump, an outside entry and make all kinds of concrete repairs. 194pp., 257 illus.

#623 HOW TO REPAIR, REFINISH AND REUPHOLSTER FURNITURE

Learn to apply first aid to ailing furniture. Reglue joints, replace webbing, bent and broken springs, caning and cane webbing. Everything you need to know from tacks to tools. Directions also explain how to build a studio bed with a nylon cord spring, decorate furniture with provincial trim, make picture frames, etc. 98pp., 138 illus.

#630 HOW TO BUILD SPORTSMAN'S REVOLVING STORAGE CABINET

Directions simplify building a glass enclosed gun cabinet, wall racks and a 24 x 72″ revolving cabinet that stores everything from guns to clothing. Learn to make what others want to buy. 98pp., 121 illus.

#632 HOW TO BUILD A VACATION OR RETIREMENT HOUSE

The perfect house for a vacation or retirment. One story with full basement provides two bedrooms and an amazing amount of useable living space. When built without a basement, it contains a bedroom, kitchen, bathroom and living room. An economical solution to today's housing costs. 194pp., 170 illus.

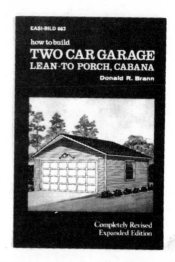

#663 HOW TO BUILD A TWO CAR GARAGE, LEAN-TO PORCH, CABANA

Building a garage can prove to be a richly rewarding experience. Letters from readers who built this garage confirm the task altered their outlook on life. Many who build turn it into an income producing singles apartment. 130pp., 142 illus.

#668 BRICKLAYING SIMPLIFIED

All who seek income, peace of mind, an economical solution to a costly problem or employment in a trade where opportunity is unlimited, find this book a real guide to better living. It explains how to lay bricks, a wall, walk, veneer a house, build a barbecue, etc. It turns amateurs into pros. 146pp., 212 illus.

#669 HOW TO BUILD BIRDHOUSES AND BIRD FEEDERS

Encouraging a child to build feeders and birdhouses can stimulate a lifetime interest in woodworking. Full size patterns not only simplify building but also insure success. Helping a child turn a piece of wood into a useable and saleable article builds instant self confidence. 66pp., 86 illus.

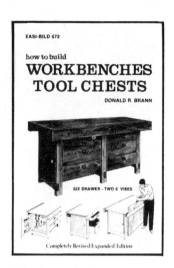

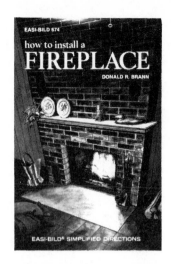

#672 HOW TO BUILD WORKBENCHES

To economically solve costly repairs and improvements, every home, apartment and place of business needs a workbench. This encourages those who build one to build others for resale. Simplified directions show how to build 6' workbenches, with a 6' vise on one or both sides, big drawers and tool compartments, to foldaway wall benches that require a minimum of floor space. 180pp., 250 illus., plus a full size foldout pattern.

#674 HOW TO INSTALL A FIREPLACE

Everyone who wants to install a woodburning stove, build a brick fireplace or install a prefabricated metal fireplace and chimney, will find all the direction they need. Installing a chimney completely within or recessed flush with an outside wall is clearly explained and illustrated. 242pp., 354 illus.

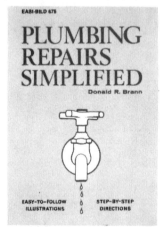

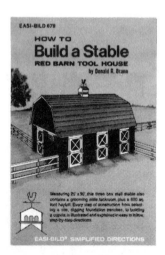

#675 PLUMBING REPAIRS SIMPLIFIED

Homeowners who dislike having their budget and peace of mind destroyed by a faulty plumbing fixture find this book helps save time, temper and money. Everyone who has learned to bake a cake or drive a car can easily replace parts and make repairs like a pro. Read, learn, then do what directions suggest and see how much more living you get out of life. 194pp., 820 illus.

#679 HOW TO BUILD A STABLE AND RED BARN TOOL HOUSE

Measuring 20 x 30', this three box stall stable is easy to build while it makes a dream come true. Every step of construction, from having a reason to build (to create an individual and not a joiner), selecting a site, to building the cupola, is explained, illustrated and simplified. Directions also simplify building an 8 x 10' or larger red barn tool house. 178pp., 197 illus.

#680 HOW TO BUILD A ONE CAR GARAGE, CARPORT, CONVERT A GARAGE INTO A STABLE

Building a one car garage with ample space for a workshop, or turning a one car garage into a two box stall stable is clearly explained. Directions tell how to raise a garage to obtain needed headroom, build a carport, lean-to toolhouse and a cupola. 146pp., 181 illus.

#682 HOW TO ADD AN EXTRA BATHROOM

This complete, easy to read guide to home plumbing helps make a dream come true for only the cost of fixtures. In easy to follow directions, it tells how to make the installation and save a bundle. Those who don't want to do any plumbing discover sizeable savings can be effected by preparing the area, then having a plumber make the installation. Read, learn, save. 162pp., 200 illus.

#683 CARPETING SIMPLIFIED

Laying carpet in your home can provide the experience needed to do the same work for others. This book explains how a pro performs each step in words and pictures every reader can easily follow. Every type of carpeting, over any kind of floor, with or without padding, is explained, illustrated and simplified. Directions explain how to carpet stairs, install protective under the carpet electronic alarm mats, and much, much more. 178pp., 223 illus.

#684 HOW TO TRANSFORM A GARAGE INTO LIVING SPACE

Transforming a garage into a living-bedroom, with a kitchen and bathroom, can provide a safe and economical solution to a costly nursing home problem. It can also become an important income producer. Step-by-step directions assume the reader has never done any of this work and explains every step. 130pp., 139 illus.

#685 HOW TO REMODEL BUILDINGS

With abandoned big city housing units available to all who are willing to rehabilitate and occupy same, this book explains how tenants can become landlords with only an investment of time and effort. It tells how to turn an abandoned multi-family building, store, garage or warehouse into rentable housing. Every step explained and illustrated. Read and learn how to become a homeowner without spending a lot of money. 258pp., 345 illus.

#690 HOW TO BUILD BARS

Building a bar offers a fun way to furnish a recreation room. Learning to build a straight, L-shaped or any of the seven bars described provides an easy way to start a part or full time business. Doing something today you didn't know how to do yesterday broadens one's sphere of activity. 162pp., 195 illus.

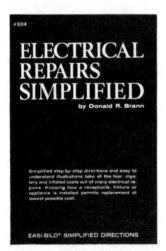

#694 ELECTRICAL REPAIRS SIMPLIFIED

Learning to economically make electrical repairs not only generates peace of mind, but also income in your spare time. This book takes the fear, mystery and inflated cost out of many troublesome repairs. A special feature explains how to install wiring in a dollhouse. 134pp., 218 illus.

#695 HOW TO INSTALL
PROTECTIVE ALARM DEVICES

Recapture peace of mind by securely protecting all doors and windows with professional alarm devices. Learn how to discourage a break-in with magnetic contacts that automatically trigger a telephone dialer to the police, sound a loud alarm bell, instantly detect movement with easy to install radar. A layman's guide to professionally installed electronic protection. 130pp., 146 illus.

206

#696 ROOFING SIMPLIFIED
This "business of your own" book turns amateurs into professional roofers. Learn to repair or replace an asphalt, wood or slate roof; apply roll roofing, make a roofer's safety harness, walk and work on a roof with no fear of falling, plus much more. 130pp., 168 illus.

#697 FORMS, FOOTINGS, FOUNDATIONS, FRAMING, STAIR BUILDING
This book tells every reader how to get into the building industry. Whether you build your own house, buy a prefab or want a career in building, this book tells everything you need to know about forms, footings, foundations, framing and stair building. 210pp., 310 illus.

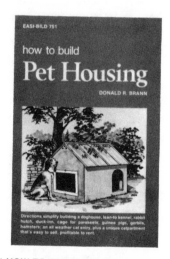

#751 HOW TO BUILD PET HOUSING
Encourage all who love pets to build the shelter each needs. Learn how to build a doghouse, lean-to kennel, rabbit hutch, duck-inn, parakeet cage, an all weather cat entry, plus a unique catpartment that's easy to sell, easy to rent. 178pp., 252 illus.

#753 HOW TO BUILD DOLLHOUSES & FURNITURE
To create a memory a little girl will never forget, build one of the three dollhouses offered in this book. Those searching for a part or full time money making hobby find a ready market for dollhouses. Full size patterns simplify making fourteen pieces of dollhouse furniture. 194pp., 316 illus.

207

#754 HOW TO BUILD OUTDOOR FURNITURE
Easy to follow step-by-step directions, plus a big foldout full size pattern, simplify tracing and cutting all parts to exact shape required. Learn how to build curved back lawn chairs, a matching settee, four passenger lawn glider, a chaise on wheels and much, much more. 130pp., 174 illus, plus full size pattern.

#756 SCROLL SAW PROJECTS
Helping everyone, a child or retiree, successfully turn a piece of wood into a handsome, useable and saleable article, builds the ego. This book insures success. 27 full size patterns permit tracing all parts, then assembling each in exact position shown on pattern. 130pp., 146 illus.

#757 HOW TO BUILD A KAYAK
Simplified directions and full size frame patterns permit building this extremely light yet sturdy kayak to three different lengths, 14 3″, 16 9″, or 18 0″. It can easily be carried on a cartop rack and used by one or two adults. Patterns insure cutting each frame to exact size required. This book includes full size patterns for all frames.

#758 HOW TO MODERNIZE A KITCHEN, BUILD BASE AND WALL CABINETS, POLE TYPE FURNITURE
Of special interest to every homeowner who appreciates the convenience and long term Capital Gains of a completely modernized kitchen. 210pp., 263 illus.

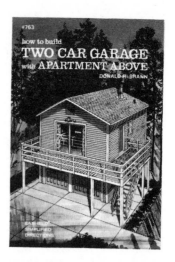

#761 HOW TO BUILD COLONIAL FURNITURE

Building colonial reproductions can provide hours of complete escape. You not only obtain furniture at a fraction of retail cost, but also enjoy every hour. Easy to follow directions and full size patterns simplify building a cobbler's bench, hutch cabinet, blanket chest, under the eaves rope bed, wall cabinet and other useful pieces. 12 colonial reproductions are offered. 258pp., 342 illus.

#763 HOW TO BUILD A TWO CAR GARAGE WITH APARTMENT ABOVE

All who seek an economical solution to a costly housing problem should read this book. It explains how to build a two car, two story garage. Directions also explain how to add a second story apartment to an existing garage. Space above provides a living, bedroom, kitchen and bathroom. Ideal for a single or couple. 194pp., 226 illus.

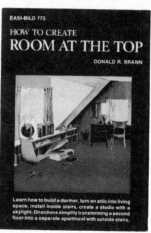

#771 TOYMAKING AND CHILDREN'S FURNITURE SIMPLIFIED

As every reader soon discovers, toymaking possesses a certain magic. Turning a piece of lumber into a whimsical rocking horse with a personality captures a child's imagination, triggers an interest in woodworking long before they have any idea how it was made. This book simplifies building 17 different toys and children's furniture. 194pp., 330 illus., plus a big foldout full size pattern.

#773 HOW TO CREATE ROOM AT THE TOP

If you need one or more extra bedrooms, or an income producing apartment with outside stairs, this book explains how to make like magic. Every step, from building a dormer, installing a skylight, building and installing inside and outside stairs to a second floor, is explained and illustrated. 162pp., 239 illus.

209

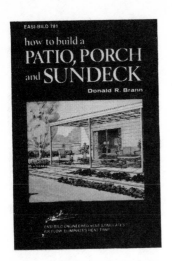

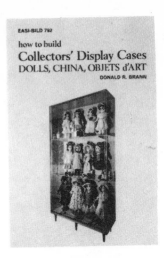

#781 HOW TO BUILD A PATIO, PORCH AND SUNDECK

Simplified directions take all the inflated cost out of building a front or back porch, a patio to length and width specified or to size desired, a carport and sundeck. Every step, from laying footings to installation of railings, is illustrated. Directions also explain how to make screens, porch repairs, swimming pool enclosure and much more. 146pp., 220 illus.

#792 HOW TO BUILD COLLECTORS' DISPLAY CASES

Learn to build handsome, clear acrylic, museum quality, floor, table top and wall display cabinets. These provide the perfect way to display every kind of possession from dolls, china, figurines, etc. Retailers buy these cases for store use and for resale. 194pp., 229 illus.

#804 HOW TO BUILD BOOKCASES AND STEREO CABINETS

Takes all the mystery and over ⅔ the cost out of building bookcases and cabinets to fill any available space. 194pp., 232 illus.

#850 HOW TO FIND A JOB, START A BUSINESS

Of special interest to teens, retirees and anyone who wants to earn extra income.

#811 HOW TO BUILD GREENHOUSES — WALK-IN, WINDOW, SUNHOUSE, GARDEN TOOL HOUSE

Of special interest to everyone who enjoys the fun and relaxation of growing plants the year round. The sunhouse appeals to sun lovers who enjoy winter sunbathing. 210pp., 229 illus.

#600 COMPLETE EASI-BILD CATALOG

Illustrates Easi-Bild home repair and improvement Books and Full Size Patterns.